BLACKROOTS SCIENCE

VOLUME 2

THE UNPUBLISHED EMAILS

MODIMONCHO

First Printing: 2019

ISBN 978-1-7923-1425-4

Blackroots Science Publications
California, United States of America

Printed in the United States.

www.blackrootscience.com
blackrootwisdom@gmail.com

Ordering Information:
Special discounts are available on quantity purchases by corporations, associations, educators, and others. For details, contact the publisher at:
blackrootwisdom@gmail.com

CONTENTS

Blackroots Science Volume 2 is a publication of the email correspondences between Brother Blackroots and certain people. These writings were left out of the first book in order to make it a convenient size. They are now published and made available to a few, and to make sure these teachings do not get lost.

1

THE SACREDNESS OF
FOOD

To our ancient ancestors, the entire creation is sacred. Everything they do is imbued with this sacredness, including the act of eating. They know that all things in nature have more than one purpose

2. So even though they realize that the primary purpose of eating is to nourish the body to keep it alive, they also recognize that there are other purposes besides nourishment.

3. This does not mean that they downplay the value of nourishment because it is just as important as

the rest. Everyone knows that without nourishment the body will not live long.

4. Knowing all this, then you can understand why to them eating is like a ritual. It is never performed absent-mindedly the way you see some people do today - eating while driving cars, or rushing through their meal so they can go do other 'more important things'.

5. Or just eating casually all day long, where some people do it so absent-mindedly that you will hear the person say, "where did my hot dog go?", not even remembering that he already ate it.

6. That type of absent-minded consumption of food is an indication that we have forgotten that food has other purposes for us besides pleasure and nourishment.

7. Of course there is nothing wrong with getting pleasure out of eating. That is why God put different pleasant tastes in many varieties of foods so that we can derive pleasure from eating while we nourish our bodies.

8. But to eat only for pleasure will always lead to unhealthy habits such as over-eating and eating

foods that are bad for our bodies. This in turn will lead to an unhealthy body and eventually to premature death following painful illnesses.

9. The ancients are able to avoid all of these pitfalls because they are taught the other purposes of food. So eating is a sacred ritual that they perform with as much attention as any other important task in their lives.

10. As I have mentioned before many times the ancients eat only once every three days. This allows their metabolism to completely process the food with maximum efficiency and not allow for the accumulation of excess poisons in their cells.

11. Also, the three day schedule enables their body to convert all, or almost all, of the food into useful energy, both on the physical and spiritual level. Food does indeed have a spiritual component to it that nourishes our various spiritual bodies as well as our minds.

12. As you know the society is organized into 72,000 towns of about 14,000 people each all over the world.

13. Now, the 14,000 or so people in the town divide themselves into 'neighborhood groups', for lack of a better word.

14. These groups consist of about 90-100 people each, and there are 144 of these groups in each town. The groups are made up of close neighbors of about 50 households who all share a single dining hall.

15. So there are 144 of these dining halls in every town (except when there are children around, then they build more dining halls to accommodate them).

16. They eat together in these large dining halls every three days. Each group has its own 3-day time-table, so a third of the 144 groups (48 groups) will eat, say, on the first day of the week, then another third on the second day, and the last third on the third day, then the first third again on the fourth day and so on.

17. They do not have situations like we have today where you see individuals eating by themselves, or individual families eating by themselves in their house.

18. To them it is a delight and a great pleasure to meet with the other 100 people in their neighborhood every three days and enjoy a meal together.

19. Basically, the men in the group take turns collecting food from the central town market. And of course it is completely free.

20. They give their food order to the market custodians in the morning and pick up the food later in the day. Every three days, men from the group will row their boats to the market and pick up their food order.

21. After the men collect and bring the food back, all food preparation and cooking is done by women.

22. At other times when there are children around, they build a separate dining hall next to the main hall where the children eat their meals every day, up to three times a day.

23. Every three days when the adults have their meal, they will eat together with the children in the main dining hall.

24. Obviously not every member of the neighborhood group will be present at every meal. People visit friends or family, or go away on work or study for a few days, and sometimes for long periods of time. Plus they also entertain visitors from out of town now and then.

25. So even though their three-day eating schedule is followed meticulously most of the time, it is not 100% rigid. Sometimes, for instance when they are out in the field and someone sees delicious wild fruits, they will go ahead and eat some right there, especially if they want to find out if it is something they want to take back to their farms to cultivate.

26. Also when they visit friends and find them to be on a different 3-day time-table than they, they will adjust theirs to fit that of their hosts for as long as they stay there.

27. Therefore it happens many times that a person, having eaten the day before, will visit friends in another town the next day and find that they are having their meal later that day.

28. Since it is never a polite thing to decline an invitation to dinner, he will join them; the result being that he ends up eating two days in a row.

29. This does not disrupt their health in the slightest. The fact that they adhere to a regular 3-day eating schedule the vast majority of the time, makes their bodies so perfectly healthy that breaking the pattern occasionally has no adverse effects whatsoever.

30. As I was saying earlier, there are other purposes to eating food besides nourishment. In order to fulfill these other purposes, women are taught in their women's rituals about the different types of foods and what other purposes they serve.

31. All people are taught in a general sense about this, but in the women's rituals they extend the topic to cover every aspect of it, especially its spiritual components.

32. All adult women are familiar with it and are food experts. They prepare the right types of foods suitable for each and every individual in their group.

33. The women have the ability to discern the spiritual needs of each and every member at any particular time. So when they prepare the food order, they take into account the physical as well as

the spiritual condition of each member at the time, and what it will be three or more days later.

34. As a result, the food that is brought back from the market every three days is different. This is also dictated by the season of the year, as some foods are available only during particular seasons. Nevertheless, they are so good at this that they manage to fulfill the needs of each and every member without having to consult them.

35. The way they do it is by studying the auras of the people, and they can tell what physical and spiritual condition they are in. Then they are able to determine what particular foods they will need to keep their physical and spiritual bodies in perfect health.

36. When a person has a certain amount and type of energy in his/her body, the aura will reflect it in a precise way. Not only that, but as the person thinks about his/her plans for the next week or so, the amount and type of energy that will be needed to fulfill those expectations is also precisely reflected in the aura.

37. Being masters at reading the aura, the women can then tell what a person's nutritional needs will

be for the coming several days.   They use this information to compose their food order which they then give to the men.

38. They do the same with visitors.   When visitors are expected, the women will read their aura remotely, before they arrive, and include the results of that information in the food order.

39. Such perfect coordination results in each and every dining experience being not only a pleasure, but also very satisfying health-wise for every person.

40. The women take turns cooking every three days - it requires 4 men to pick up food from the market, and 4 women to prepare and cook it for a hundred or so people.

41. Their food preparation system and cooking implements are far more sophisticated than ours today, such that it does not require many people. At the end of the meal the women who cooked are always heaped with genuine praises about how good the food was. This happens every single time.

42. At the end of each meal, as the people remain for a while longer in the dining hall talking, the 4

women who will be cooking next will take a minute or two to study the auras of everyone. The people are all in a happy mood at that moment, having been well fed; they are relaxed and each one's aura is at its brightest - literally begging to be read.

43. After reading their auras, they will retain this information, and a day or two later use it to compile the next food order. This will be repeated like clock-work every three days.

44. As you can imagine, this takes all the stress out of preparing, cooking and eating food. People never have to worry about where their next meal is coming from or what types of food they need to eat on any given day to maintain their health. This is all taken care of with perfect coordination and execution.

45. It leaves them with all the time they need to take care of other things in their perfect lives; to work, to study, to socialize and ultimately to fulfill their destinies.

46. Now I will talk a little bit about their farming techniques, as well as their food distribution methods.

47. Only the two youngest generations engage in farming and food distribution activities. This includes all the people under 1,000 years of age - none of them have taken part in any of the Great Rituals - and the generation above them, those under 2,000 years of age, and they have completed the first Great Ritual but not the second.

48. Most of the work is done by the younger generation, the older one being there mostly to teach them how to farm, and to coordinate the food distribution process. When there are children around, they too are taken to the farms to teach them at the earliest possible age.

49. They have large plots of land dedicated specifically to farming and growing fruit trees. As I mentioned before, each country is divided into 6 clans, and each clan into 100 districts, each district being made up of 10 towns, or approximately 144,000 people.

50. Every district has a large plot for farms and orchards. That means there are farmlands in every suitable part of the country, enabling them to grow every type of food according to climate.

51. They trade some of their produce among the 12 Tribes, and then distribute the traded food to the clan capitals. From there they are sorted according to the needs of the districts, and then distributed to the district capitals.

52. Then each district will combine all the traded foods they receive, with the locally produced foods and distribute them to the town markets.

53. Once there, men will come in their boats or other means of transportation and collect food every day, made ready for them according to their food orders. When there are no children or young adults under 28, each neighborhood group will send its 4 men to pick up food every three days.

54. But when children are around, the food production is increased extensively, and the men go to the market every day - that includes young boys old enough to row a boat, while young girls that are old enough take turns helping the women to prepare the food.

55. The people in each neighborhood group include members of all seven generations. Remember that at all times (under normal circumstances) there are always 7 generations of people on earth - the

youngest being under 1,000 years of age, then those 1,000 - 2,000 years, and so on up to the oldest generation 6,000 years and older.

56. All of them are there in every town. Once a couple builds their own house in a certain town, they live there for the rest of their lives. They never move to another house or another town and make a new home.

57. Only newly married couples move, usually the woman moving to the town of her husband in the present patriarchal society. After settling down, they will live in that same house for the rest of their lives.

58. Every couple builds their own house with the help of their neighbors. When a family patriarch and matriarch ascend, the home plot of land they occupied will now be occupied by the married couple next in line for a new home.

59. Usually the patriarch and matriarch will not ascend until their youngest descendents are over 77 years old. Only then does a plot of land become available.

60. In the meantime, the young married couple builds a small house on the land occupied by the man's parents. Each family lives on a large plot of land, close to 4 acres for small families with 2 children or less, and larger for big families with more than 2 children. So there is plenty of room to build more houses.

61. Since they get married at the age of about 14 to 18 years old, they will continue to live in their own house on the same land with their parents until they are over 77 years old.

62. Then a plot of land becomes available when a senior couple ascends. They do not have children until they are over 1,000 years old and have completed the first Great Ritual.

63. The young couple, when they eventually get their own plot, will then remove all the structures that were built on that plot, and renew the land using certain methods they were taught.

64. They then build their main house and surrounding structures on that land, and live there for 7,000 years or longer, until they too ascend. The only time people move out of their towns is at the end of the 700,000 year Elder cycle, when the

entire earth is rearranged. As I said before, this happened about 150,000 years ago.

65. And so you will find every generation represented in every neighborhood group, and they all contribute to the dining work - the women cooking and the men picking up the food from the market and cleaning after dinner.

66. But all the older men, those above 3,000 years of age, always joke that they don't have time to be rowing around in boats to pick up food. They say they did that enough when they were young.

67. What they do is when their turn comes, they go to the market remotely with their minds, de-materialize the food in the containers, and re-materialize it at its destination. And they always play games with the cooking women.

68. When the women come in to cook and find the storage room containers empty, they know right away that it's the 'old-timers' playing tricks again. So they wait for a few seconds, and then the bins instantly fill with food right before them.

69. All the men, when their turn comes, get the food order from the women and relay it

telepathically to the market custodians the morning of pick-up day. There are always between 9 and 12 people working at the market when it is open.

70. They all receive the food orders telepathically. When they come to work in the morning, the first thing they do is come together and make a combined telepathic announcement to the whole town that they are ready to receive food orders.

71. Within about a minute or two, they receive 48 food orders for that day, from 48 different groups. As I said there are 144 groups, and every day a third of them, 48 groups, will eat dinner.

72. The food orders all come in nearly at once. The whole process takes less than 5 minutes. The people do not use a writing system (but the containers of each neighborhood group are permanently marked with symbols and colors).

73. They mentally record all the orders, about 4 or 5 orders per custodian, and then proceed to fill the empty containers that are sitting on the dock, that were exchanged for full ones three days earlier when the men came in to pick up food.

74. Their system of filling the food orders is simply amazing. All the food-stuffs have been previously sorted and stacked on the market shelves - different types of food in appropriately sized, uniform containers. The containers are made of a certain type of manufactured crystal, with a sealing lid.

75. The food is kept at a constant temperature in the storage rooms, whose walls are built with thick stone. The most perishable foods such as fruits and vegetables, will stay fresh in these crystal containers for up to 7 years. But they don't keep food that long.

76. Food that is rotated from the oldest stock and taken to the dining halls will usually have been sitting in storage in the town market for about 7-10 days.

77. Before then, it will have been in storage at the district capital for another 7-10 days, and before then, if it is traded food, will have been in the clan capital storage rooms for another 7-10 days, and before then at the farm storage area for several more days.

78. So it is in storage and distribution for a total of 20 to 40 days, depending on whether it is traded or local food.

79. I'm referring specifically to perishable foods. They are stored in these crystal containers immediately after harvest, and 40 days later they taste as fresh as food that was harvested that day.

80. Grains, herbs and other foods that are not easily perishable are in the storage/distribution cycle longer, being stored in much larger containers. They are transferred to smaller metal containers made of silver or gold when they are ready to be picked up.

81. When they are ready to fill the food orders, the market custodians sit in a round room in the middle of the market place. The room is surrounded by twelve storage rooms, with variously sorted foods of all kinds.

82. The custodians then bring the food order lists up in their minds, and as soon as they do this, the right number and kind of containers of food dematerializes out of the storage rooms and into the containers at the dock.

83. They are able to do it instantly, without having to locate the different foods because they already know where every single container is located, and the type and amount of food in it.

84. They effortlessly memorized it all when they were unloading the ship and stocking the market shelves in the storage rooms at the time the food was delivered from the district capital.

85. What is even more amazing about the process is that each person fills his or her orders, 4 or 5 of them, simultaneously.   The entire process takes them less than a minute to complete.

86. They are usually at the market for about 10 to 20 minutes only, and most of that time is spent just sitting talking while they wait for all the custodians to arrive, because they all work as one.

87. The actual work, taking orders and filling them, all takes about 6 or 7 minutes. Then they are done for the day and leave.

88. The only time they are there longer is when new shipments come in every 10 days or so. Then they work at the market for about an hour, restocking the shelves.

89. When the men come in to pick up their food, there is usually no one inside the market. They find their containers full of food waiting for them on the dock.

90. They exchange their clean, empty containers for full ones, then linger around the dock for a while talking to others, and then head back. They get to talk to the market workers only once every 10 days when they find them unloading the ship.

91. Now, market workers are not the same people at all times. Every adult in town does this job (as well as many others). They take turns working in the market just like they do with the other dining work.

92. Their farming methods are simple, labor intensive methods. They do use animals for some of the farm work, such as plowing the land. They have very intricate and highly efficient irrigation systems that rely on the fountains, rivers and streams that abundantly criss-cross all of their countries.

93. Farming is perhaps the hardest work they do. As I said, they start as children and do it intensively for about a thousand years. After that, they no longer engage in the hard work, but go mainly to teach the new generation that came after them, who will now perform all the hard work.

94. When it comes time to harvest, they make use of what they call their 'harvesting crystals'. These are specially made crystals that they use to transmit images that help them to visualize the separation of the food from the rest of the plant, or the fruits from the trees.

95. They use this visualization process to de-materialize the harvests instantly; and I will try to describe their harvesting technology.

96. The process is similar to that used in the markets in that it is also a de-materialization process. The difference is that the crops on a farm-field or the fruits on a tree are not neatly placed like stock on shelves where they can all be visualized easily and transferred by this process.

97. Every plant and tree is different, and the food is located randomly all around the tree by nature, so it would be especially complicated to try and visualize every single fruit on the tree, and every single grain on the stalk to de-materialize it and separate it from the rest of the plant.

98. There are older people that can actually do this, but according to custom they do not use their powers for such work.

99. The real reason they do not is because there are certain side benefits that are very important for the young people, that can only be learnt efficiently when they use certain types of technologies, and their crystal technology falls in that class.

100. Every person has to master it before they can advance and gain higher powers that use only the mind.

101. The same holds true for the type of hard work they have to perform on their farms in preparation for the harvesting season, as well as the use of animals.

102. They could easily make machinery that can do all their farm work, but then they would lose other benefits, mostly spiritual ones, that they gain by working on nature directly with their own hands when they are young.

103. To use the harvesting crystals, they place them in the field and make a recorded image of all the plants to be harvested. The crystals record an image of each and every plant in crystal-clear, life-like detail.

104. The way the crystals record images is not by using light the way modern cameras do. They record the actual electromagnetic properties of an object, which means they record equally well in the light, in the dark, or on objects that are hidden behind others. The farthest object will be as clear as the nearest.

105. As I have said before, everything in existence has a unique frequency of vibration. The crystals record all these unique frequencies that are within their focus.

106. Their range of focus can extend for many miles, depending on the size and type of crystal. They are not very large, the largest being only about the size of an average-sized book such as a bible, and the smallest being about the size of a matchbox.

107. For a large field, they will place one book-sized crystal on its stand in the middle of the field. The crystal will cover the entire field and produce a recorded image of each and every plant on the farm. The images are transmitted instantly to the central room of the farm storage building.

108. Scientists in that room will study all the images for a few minutes, taking samples. The transmitted

recording includes all the sensory properties of the plant and crop, meaning the texture, the smell and taste, etc.

109. They wear a certain type of crystal on a bracelet on their forearm that enables then to sample the texture, taste, smell etc of the entire field of crops in just a few seconds.

110. The best crops will stand out among the rest by presenting a more perfect symphony of vibration, sort of like listening to many songs at the same time and then hearing the ones that have a superior quality stand out among the rest.

111. These crops are automatically singled out on the recording directly by the minds of the scientists, so as to distinguish them from the rest. They will be saved and used for seeds in the next season.

112. When that stage is completed (and it only takes a couple of minutes) then they go to the next stage which is to separate the grains from the rest of the plant. This separation occurs on the imagery only, it is not yet an actual separation out on the farm.

113. The crystal is programmed in such a way that it can 'tell' the difference between a grain and the

rest of the plant, because they have clearly distinct frequencies of vibration.

114. Upon receiving a mental command, it will produce a new set of images that shows only the grains, with the rest of the plant not showing. At this point, the scientists are ready to go to the final step which is to de-materialize the grains and move them into their containers in the storage rooms.

115. They start first by de-materializing the seed-crops that they singled out earlier, and store them first, then the others that are to be used for food, and store those in their appropriate places.

116. Harvesting vegetables is similar. They make an image distinction between the edible part of the plant, and the rest of the plant by programming the frequencies into the crystal.

117. The crystal then presents them with images made up only of the edible part, not showing the rest of the plant. Then they de-materialize only what shows on the images in the room, thus separating the edible part of the plant from the rest.

118. In a similar way, they harvest the fruits from their orchards. First they separate the seeds from

the best tasting fruits, to use them in the next planting.

119. The crystal, when recording an image, does not capture only the exterior of the object like a modern camera. It captures the entire vibrational symphony that makes up the fruit.

120. So it can be programmed to separate the skin and meat of the fruit from the seed, and present an image of the seed only.

121. When the scientists focus their attention on these images of the seeds, and start the dematerialization process in their minds, the actual seeds that are out on the orchard will be cleanly separated from the rest of the fruit.

122. The difference between the best crops and the rest is very marginal. What the people eat, were last season's best crops, and the best seeds that are saved this season, will be regular crops in coming seasons.

123. But over time, this selection makes each plant more perfect, even though the difference is barely noticeable over the short run.

124. In the long run, the farm plants evolve slowly but steadily partly because of human cultivation, until the end when they will reach the pinnacle of their evolution and become absolutely perfect.

125. They transport their produce on large cargo ships and other means of transportation. I will talk only about their ships. These large ships are self-operated with no one on board. They are guided along the canals and rivers by a programmed crystal with a set path.

126. Their man-made canals and waterways are extremely well-built with clean, flowing, drinkable water. They are lined along the sides and bottom with marble and other hard stones.

127. They are fed with water from the natural fountains, rivers and other streams. In some towns they are connected directly to large lakes that are in elevated areas.

128. At the entrance to the main canal that feeds all the other canals at the edge of town, they place a type of magnetic gate. This is a specially designed magnetic field suspended between two crystals. They fine-tune the way this field operates by programming the crystals.

129. Generally, they are programmed to let only water go through the magnetic gate, which purifies it as it goes through. The programming is very complex.

130. It will allow only specific minerals through that are flowing with the water, while diverting others away from the main canal back to the stream via a separate, smaller canal. The gate will also prevent any kind of debris such as leaves and twigs and mud from entering. It will also let certain types of small fish and other water life through, but not others.

131. The magnetic field extends from the gate along the length of the canals, providing a type of cover over the entire canal system. This prevents all other debris from falling into the canal, such as falling leaves, dust, insects, etc.

132. Because of this, the canals never need cleaning. They maintain themselves in pristine condition for thousands of years. The lining stones also never need replacing for the entire life of the canal system.

133. The only type of maintenance performed on the system is to ensure that they always have an adequate supply of water to the inlet. Sometimes the streams can get diverted by natural

circumstances, in which case they would dig and reroute it accordingly.

134. The people are very fond of water. You will see them swimming in the canals every day. In all the towns that have canals (there are some that do not, that use other means of transportation) the main canals are about 50 feet wide, with narrower canals connecting to them.

135. The main canals are meant for the large cargo ships. The connecting narrower canals are used by smaller boats such as the ones they use to go to the market.

136. Connected to the sides of some of the canals are large swimming pools, about 200 feet by 200 feet where the people swim. Each town has about 40 of these large pools. Even the towns that do not have a canal system have their swimming pools.

137. The children will not only swim in the swimming pools, but they will go into the traffic lanes of the canals and swim there also, especially the main ship-canals.

138. When they see a cargo ship coming, some children will just stay in its path to see what will happen. This is a game they like to play.

139. They know that the cargo ships are unmanned, and they do this just to see what the ship will do. All ships and boats, even the smaller ones, are equipped with a child-proof system that will stop the ship if there is any object in its path.

140. Even though the children are told this, they still play this game. When they see that the ship indeed comes to a stop, and will not move until they get out of the way, then they move and thereafter lose interest in the game.

141. It seems that all children do it. The adults just ignore them, knowing that they will only do it once or twice and then lose interest, because they too did it when they were children.

142. One thing they are unable to do though is to approach within 10 feet of the ship. The ships are covered by a field that prevents anyone from advancing beyond its 10-foot perimeter.

143. Only mature people, those who have gone through puberty, are able to disengage the field and

board the ship by using a mental command, and they never give this command to children.

144. When the children become very curious and want to board the ship, a couple of adults or older teenagers will take them to the market place, where the ship is headed. After it docks, they will take them aboard so they can look at it.

145. This happens a lot when there are children around. But because for the greater majority of time there are no children on earth, the unmanned ships are free to go on their way without any trouble.

146. There are bridges located at regular intervals for crossing the canals. These are not elevated bridges. They are 'mechanical' bridges that advance and retract from both sides of the canal.

147. They are made from giant slabs of very light but hard stones. Each bridge consists of two long slabs, one on either side of the canal, that are about 14 feet wide and 50 feet long.

148. Each stone is laid lengthwise in a trench near the water's edge. The trench is about 10 feet deep and 50 feet long, to take the whole length of the slab.

149. The slabs then slide into the water toward each other until they touch to form a bridge. The top of the stone is only about a foot above the water level, and the water level itself is about 2 feet below ground level.

150. When they are fully in and touching, the water will continue to flow under the stones. Only a third of the length of the stone is in the water. The remaining two-thirds is still supported in the trench by its own weight to prevent the stone from tipping over.

151. Once they touch they are magnetically locked to each other so that you can even put a large weight on them. But generally they do no take any large weights; they are used just for walking to cross the canals.

152. I want to describe these bridges in detail because there is something about them that has to do with the children that is very fascinating.

153. When the bridge is fully retracted, the stone lies buried in its trench, and two-thirds of its length is totally underground covered with vegetation, usually short grass. This vegetation is actually planted in soil right on top of the stone.

154. The front one-third of its length is left bare and visible - that is the part of it that enters the water. When it slides and advances into the water, it takes the covering vegetation with it, and leaves the trench gaping wide open behind.

155. When a person wants to cross the bridge, he approaches any part of the stone. As soon as he steps on top of it and remains still for about 2 or 3 seconds, or walks along its length towards the water for about 2 or 3 seconds, then the stone starts gently sliding forward.

156. The other stone across the water also starts sliding until they both meet in the middle of the canal. After the person crosses and steps off the stone, they both begin to retract back into their trenches.

157. As I said, each stone leaves about a 17 foot length of the trench gaping wide open when it slides to form the bridge; but it is not possible to enter this trench.

158. It is covered with a magnetic field that is similar to that which covers the perimeter of the ship. But you can clearly see the sides and bottom of this wide, 10-foot deep hole.

159. Now, what the children do is as soon as this hole is exposed, they jump on top of it, trying to get into the hole. They will jump up and down for a while, then come running to join the others crossing the bridge, and run past them to the other side and jump up and down on that trench as well. They do this almost every time they cross the bridge.

160. The slabs used to cross the main canals are much bigger. They are about 30 feet wide and over 75 feet long. They are cut differently than the small bridges.

161. The back two-thirds of their length that is covered with vegetation is about 30 feet deep, while the front part that advances into the water is about 15 feet deep.

162. The canals are dug extra deep at the bridge crossings to accommodate the stones. The front part of these larger ones also has round holes in them to allow water to flow through when the bridge is connected.

163. A ship that approaches a bridge on the main canal prevents the stones from closing when it is at a distance of about 300 feet. After the ship is about

20 feet past the bridge, then the bridge can be operated again.

164. The trenches of these stones are massive. When they form a bridge, they leave an open trench behind that is 30 feet wide, 50 feet long and 30 feet deep. The children love to play on these trenches more than on the smaller ones.

165. They will even go to the main canal to operate the bridge not with the intent to cross, but just so they can run back and forth between the two trenches, jumping up and down on top of the holes, trying to fall inside.

166. When they run back and forth like that, sometimes they slip on the wet stones and fall into the water - but all of them can swim. They never get hurt though even if they hit the edge of the bridge, which does not have any side railings.

167. The reason they never get hurt is because they have a certain natural protection mechanism around their bodies that prevents any object from hurting them when it falls on them, or when they fall onto a hard surface, no matter how far they fall. I will describe this about their bodies at another time.

168. There is a very intelligent reason why they play on the trenches like that. The children, like all other people, are extremely intelligent.

169. There is no way to describe their intelligence by comparing it to modern people. Their intelligence is through the roof the moment they open their eyes and make first eye contact with their mother.

170. The reason they stop the cargo ship is because they were told the ship will stop by itself when someone is in its way. So the first thing they want to do is confirm this.

171. Not because they don't believe their parents or other adults when they tell them things - they do; but they still want to see it for themselves.

172. They are all raised this way, to investigate things for themselves and have an insatiable appetite for knowledge that lasts their whole lifetime, and is satisfied only when they become full God and know all things.

173. Once they have seen the ship stop 2 or 3 times, they naturally lose interest in this game and go onto other things. In their world, there is so much for them to discover and investigate - they will not

waste time repeating something from which they have already gained all the knowledge they can.

174. But when it comes to playing on the trenches, this they can never get enough of. All children, even modern children, are fascinated by mysterious holes and hidden rooms and tunnels and things like that. They cannot resist the urge to get inside anything that seems to be hidden.

175. So they jump up and down on the trenches hoping that someday they will be able to fall in and get to the bottom of the hole. Adults tell them all the time that one day, if they keep playing like that, they will fall into the hole, and in a way that sort of encourages them to keep doing it.

176. The adults of course are again telling them the truth, but they do not explain under what circumstances they will fall in there. But every single one of them eventually falls in, and when they do, they do no tell the other children that it happened.

177. When they eventually fall in, it always takes them by surprise. This happens to every child right around the time they reach puberty. It happens spontaneously. You will see an older child of about

11,12 or 13 still walk to the trenches once in a while and peer curiously down the hole.

178. At that age, they no longer jump up and down on top of the hole, but they will still accompany their younger siblings or friends to the trenches now and then and watch them play. Then one of these older children will approach the hole and stand on top of it, still wondering how he can enter it.

179. If it is his or her time, it will happen quickly, taking him completely by surprise. The child will find himself or herself on the floor of the trench, looking up at the other children, who are still running back and forth across the bridge screaming at the top of their voices and jumping up and down on the hole, completely ignoring him.

180. Still surprised, and now getting confused, he will continue to look up until he sees an older child standing up there, peering down at him. As he looks closer, he realizes that he is actually looking at his own body.

181. At that point, something miraculous happens. He finds himself back in his body, perfectly conscious and still peering into the hole, and at the

same time is still inside the hole, looking up at himself.

182. Then he realizes that part of his mind seems to have dissociated and entered the hole, while the rest of his mind is still with him as he is in his body. As soon as he realizes this, he is overcome by an ecstatic feeling, and for the first time, he understands what the adults meant when they kept saying that one day he will fall into the trench.

183. Right after that, the experience ends. He finds himself fully in his body. He quietly leaves the screaming children, who he can tell have no idea what just happened to him. He goes back home and tells his parents, uncle, older sister, or whichever adult he finds in his house or the house next door.

184. The adult, upon hearing this, says absolutely nothing for a moment or two. Then as if he did not even hear what the child said, he will say something like, "Why don't you take those tools over there and go to your cousin's house and help him fix his boat". Or, "Why don't you go to the garden and pick some flowers for your mother".

185. Still confused, he or she will obey and go do what the adult says. From then on, he will not say

anything to anyone else about it. Some days or even weeks will pass as if nothing happened. Then one day, one of his mentors will approach him or her and say, "You are now ready to prepare for your ritual of puberty".

186. At that point everything falls into place in his mind. He does not have any more questions or confusions about what happened. He realizes, without having been told by anyone, just from observing the way the adults are now looking at him, that this is something that happens to everyone who is approaching puberty.

187. After the day the mentor tells him that, he finds out that he can dissociate at will and enter the hole whenever he wants. He also finds out that he can enter his house and any house while still standing outside.

188. As he experiments with this new ability, he discovers its limits for someone his age. He finds out that he can remotely see only into places that are no more than about 700 feet from him. He cannot go further than that no matter how hard he tries.

189. He asks his mentor about it and is told that the ability is just starting to be born in him. It will increase after his first important ritual, the ritual of puberty. It will keep increasing until it reaches a peak, where he can see to the other side of the earth, after he completes his education at 77 years of age.

190. That explains the fascination that all children have with the trenches.

191. Now, to continue about the other purposes of eating; all the people over 77 years of age, meaning those that have completed the ritual for the creation of life, have a supernaturally intense awareness of everything they put in their bodies - especially the food and liquids they consume.

192. They have an informal ritual that everyday you will see being performed by someone somewhere. A person will go to a stream or fountain or any natural source of pure water and take some water in his hands to drink. Before drinking, he will say a certain familiar chant that everyone knows. This chant, generally speaking, can be explained like this:

193. When a person wants someone, say an aunt or uncle, to explain something important to him, then he takes the water and before drinking it, communicates telepathically with the aunt to tell her that he is about to put in his body what was once in her body.

194. To explain what they mean by that statement, it is clear that when people breathe out, some moisture comes out. Liquids also leave the body through sweating.

195. (But they sweat very little, even when doing heavy physical work. They have as part of their bodies, a natural mechanism for removing sweat and everything that is unwanted from their skin without taking a bath. This keeps their bodies clean at all times).

196. So when they breathe out and exhale some water vapor, or when sweat is evaporated from their skin, it naturally becomes part of the moisture in the air. It will either fall down as dew, or rise up to join the clouds and fall down as rain somewhere.

197. Then it may flow in a river, or water a plant somewhere, or do one of many other things that are part of the earth's water cycle. But someday - it may be a year later or many decades later - that drop of moisture that came out of the aunt's body will float down a river or stream and be captured by the person we mentioned above.

198. Unbelievable as it may sound, all the people who are over 77 years of age have the ability to pinpoint a drop of water in a stream and identify it as part of the breath of someone they know. When such a thing happens, the person who is looking to perform this ritual is alerted in his mind automatically. He is then able to concentrate and spiritually see it as it comes down the stream close to his location.

199. He will then go to the stream and wait for it, then cup it in his hands as it flows by. Then he will perform the ritual as I have described above. After saying the chant and after drinking the water, he will inform his aunt that he has done so and is now ready to receive instruction from her about the matter on which he had previously consulted her and requested her to enlighten him.

200. All that is the gist of the chant. The aunt will then meet him as soon as is convenient and proceed to teach him, knowing that he is now ready to understand what she has to offer because they are united by that particle of liquid that was once in her

body, and after being purified by nature, is now in his body.

201. This also applies to the food they eat. They are able to recognize if there is even a molecule in the food they eat that was watered with the water that was once a part of someone's body whose knowledge they seek.

202. So you can see how eating for them becomes a ritual. Not only do they enjoy the food they eat, but they enjoy if even more when the opportunity arises for one of them in the dining hall to enact this ritual at the dinner table.

203. Moreover, all of them are keenly aware that every morsel of food they eat was once a part of an ancestor of theirs no matter how long ago, whether it's only a few million years ago, or many trillions of years ago. They eat always with this type of presence of mind.

204. This is part of the reason they eat together, so they can enjoy it when one of them performs this ritual. It does not happen every single time they eat, but it happens often enough that it brings joy to the whole group.

205. This keen awareness they have about the food they eat is part of the reason why their bodies are permanently healthy.

206. They never experience any kind of food-associated discomforts such as indigestion, heart-burn or any of the discomforts we experience today because of our lack of awareness about what it is we are putting in our bodies, and more especially the absent-mindedness with which we consume our food.

2

DREAM WORK AND
THE 144,000

Yes my Brother, it is my estimation that it will all happen by the year 2014. But as you know, only the 24 Elders know the future in all its details. Nonetheless, it's still possible to make a reliable estimate based on how fast the information is being spread to Black people.

2. The way I see Blackroots Science spreading in the few years we have been doing this, I would say the 144,000 will be ready by 2014.

3. The final determining factor is the rising of the 144,000. As soon as they have all risen from self-forgetfulness, that will 'officially' signal the end of non-Black rule on earth.

4. That of course does not mean that when groups here and there declare that they are part of the 144,000 then it is done. It must be real. They must separate not only mentally, but also physically and set up their own communities where they can live independent of the white man's world, socially and economically.

5. When that is fulfilled, most definitely we will see all the other things I talked about come to pass, including the appearance of the anti-christ as well as the return of Yahweh.

6. **Can you give us some pointers or just a general idea on the best way or fast way to reach the number? What do we as individual can we do to get more people exposed to the info?**

7. There is no best or fastest way to do it. The advise that I offer everyone who asks this question is, let the material in Blackroots Science speak for

itself. The important thing is to expose as many people as you can to the book simply by telling them about it whenever you can, on the internet and in person, and making sure they know where to find it.

8. That is why I insisted when you requested to publish the book for sale to also publish a free copy either in PDF or Microsoft format. Remember I also suggested that, if at all possible, to make an audio book because not everyone likes to read.

9. You need not worry that everyone will take the free book and never buy the print copy. Many people who first take an electronic copy, will later get a print copy because people still prefer to study from a real book that they can underline and highlight.

10. Those are really the serious people who are most likely part of the 144,000. And many of them have friends and family that they know very well, and are in a better position than me and you to tell if they too are ready for this knowledge. Some of these people they live with or are their neighbors, and some are even in prisons all over the country.

11. So the dissemination of this information will have a self-increasing effect. The more people who hear about it, the quicker it will spread. And the most effective way to learn it is when you study with other people.

12. When that happens, then leaders will naturally arise among these study groups and take charge and begin to work in a practical way to carry the mission of the 144,000 forward.

13. Just keep doing the work of exposing people to it as you have been doing so well thus far. The so-called 'elect' are already all here. They just need to be exposed to this knowledge and it won't be long before they realize that this knowledge is meant for them. It is their destiny to be the future rulers of the earth.

14. The entire Black population depends on them, and they will fulfill their destiny.

15. As you know from your own experience, me and my wife have met many of you in the dream world. Presently, only a handful have advanced far enough to the point where they can remember the experience.

16. But as they continue to do the exercises in the book, especially the thought and dream exercises, then more will become conscious in their dreams, and it will then become possible for us to work with them in a lucid dream.

17. Remember, as I told you, that number is all we need.   The rest of the Black population may continue to sympathize with this evil system, thinking that it can be corrected, reformed or adjusted in some way;   as soon as that number is reached, it will have a cascading effect, starting in the mental realm and eventually filtering to the physical realm.

18. Then all Black people will finally lose all sympathy for the races.   Without it, their whole structure will fall.   At the present time it is being supported only by our sympathy.   The protection they enjoyed for 6,000 years ended back in 1914, and now only our sympathy continues to keep them in power.

19. I must confess I too I have not reached the point where I can remember the other encounters I have with you in the dream world. that one I told you about is the only one I

remember vividly. Other than that I have very vague recall. What was it about that one in particular to make it stand out? Was i doing something different?

20. I wouldn't say you were doing anything different, but I had never before seen you as calm as you were that time. It seemed to me that you had no major problems to deal with - either that or you had decided to simply put them aside and concentrate more on this.

21. See, even though we may have personal problems most of the time, it is possible to put them aside for a while - just put them out of our minds so we can concentrate better on something else.

22. It is really a waste of time and energy to worry constantly about any particular problem no matter how serious it is. When you deal with the problem, that's when you should worry about it. When you are not in a position to do anything about it, what good does it do to worry about it? You will have enough time to worry about it when the time comes to deal with it.

23. This is something that you can practice more, i.e. how to put yourself in a state of mind where you can gather all of your attention and focus it on the matter at hand.

24. When you do this, you will discover that your daily worries do not enter into your dreams as much as they used to. That enables you to separate your conscious mind from your other sub-conscious thoughts that are always with you whether you are asleep or awake.

25. If you do it enough in the waking state, it will naturally and effortlessly filter into your sleeping state. This will help you to have a worry-free, relaxed mind as you fall asleep, thus enabling you to remember your dreams better, even to become conscious while asleep and have a lucid dream.

26. **Can you tell me   a method or particular steps i can use to practice? Maybe something i can do every night to put me in a more or better state of relaxation?**

27. Sure. Of course doing the recalls just before going to sleep will help you very much to relax. You can also supplement that with a simple daily

routine, especially on those nights when you are not doing a recall.

28. Just take about 2 or 3 minutes when you go to bed to do this. Sit in a relaxed position with your head looking forward. Your hands should be relaxed by your sides or on your lap. Then close your eyes (it is better to do this in the dark, but if not possible, just closing your eyes is enough) .

29. While in this position, bring up a particularly vivid image to your mind of anything you saw that day. Hold the image continuously in your mind for 1 or 2 minutes while mentally looking at all its details.

30. It can be a flower, a house, a bird – any object that you remember vividly with all its colors (you may even prepare for this during the day by choosing something and looking at it intently to memorize its details).

31. It's not necessary to hold it for longer than 1 or 2 minutes. What this will do is still your mind, removing all other thoughts, especially if you had things at the back of your mind that you were worried about.

32. It is easier if the object is a living thing, such as an apple instead of a tennis ball, or a bird instead of a car. The reason is because when you try to bring the object into your mind, living things will 'meet you halfway', for lack of a better expression.

33. They will literally sense that you are trying to communicate with them, and will naturally move their own attention - their mind - to meet your mind. With dead objects, you have to 'carry it all the way into your attention' like a dead weight, because they cannot become conscious of the fact that you are trying to place your attention on them. I think you understand what I mean.

34. After doing this every night for several weeks, you will begin to notice that you fall into a much more relaxed state of sleep. A relaxed state of sleep is important for helping you to remember your dreams more clearly when you wake up, as well as to help you become lucid in your dreams.

35. **When I hold the image constantly for 2 minutes should i be looking at one side of it or part of it constantly the whole time?**

36. No, you may look it up and down all over, and even move your focus around and look at all its sides. As long as it remains in your mind continuously for 1 or 2 minutes, it will take all your attention away from everything else, and cause your mind to relax.

37. **Does it have to be a different object everyday?**

38. No, it can be the same object. If you find that focusing on the same object repeatedly helps you to see it more clearly, then do the same object. If you don't have much of a problem visualizing, then you can bring some variety to the process and do different objects. It's all up to you.

39. **Thank you again.**

3

THE TRUE CONCEPT OF MARRIAGE

b lkroots, You said that in ancient times people abstained from sex before marriage, and then on here you say Yakub and his soul mate had sex before marriage?

2. In ancient times what we call marriage was looked at far differently than is the case today. There were no papers to sign or people standing before an official and saying 'till death do us part' when they really don't mean it.

3. Young people, both girls and boys, underwent their rites of passage after reaching puberty. At these rites, they were taught all about sex and its two purposes, which are procreation and the attainment of divine unity.

4. After the rites, and after all the ceremonies and feasts that followed, then the boy and girl (who are no longer a boy and girl at that point, but have reached a certain level of maturity) would get together before priests and engage in their first sexual union. The priest and priestess that attend the couple would very lovingly guide them all the way through it, given the fact that this is their first time.

5. So there would not be any opportunity for embarrassment or anything like that, as sometimes happens today when young people have to find out for themselves how to engage in sex properly. They make mistakes that they cannot help due to ignorance. This can sometimes cause psychological damage which can take many years to overcome.

6. Such things did not happen back then. And there was no embarrassment experienced by the young couple in having to engage in intimacy in front of spectators. This was part of their culture.

As soon as children heard about sex, they learnt that the first sexual union of every couple would be performed before a priest and priestess whose duty is to guide them.

7. There was not even the slightest sense of perversion that is seen today where modern people would associate such an activity with group sex, or what they call orgies.

8. They understood and accepted that fact just as naturally as modern women accept the fact that their baby may be delivered by a man in a hospital, in front of spectators.

9. So the couple would then go ahead and engage in their first sexual union under those circumstances, guided all the way by the priest and priestess, until they achieve divine unity of their minds at the moment of their physical climax.

10. It did happen sometimes that they would not be able to attain divine unity the first time. Mostly that was because either the male or the female or both were not ready.

11. In that case one or both of them would undergo further ritual education for another 3 or 4 months,

or however long it took, until the priests were sure that they were ready. Then they would engage one more time in their intimate union before the priests and this time they would succeed. Their system of education was that good that if they failed the first time (which was rare), they would succeed the second time.

12. At any rate, when that successful divine union occurs, that day is regarded as their day of marriage. They are "legally" married (to use a modern word) from that time on, meaning that what was separated at conception has now become united again.

13. The wedding festival that follows months after that is simply an opportunity for the community to celebrate the first divine union of the couple.

14. Every time they re-celebrate their wedding day, whether it's their 10th anniversary, or 20th or 50th, they are not celebrating the day of their wedding festival, but rather the day of their first divine unity, which is their real marriage.

15. That is how the ancients regarded marriage.
So when Yakub and Maitseye had their wedding festival, they had already been married for several

months; their marriage having taken place in front of a priest and priestess, and having been consummated in a climax of divine unity, which is how the First Self blesses the marriage.

4

POPULATION STABILIZATION

G reetings my beloved Sister,

2. The population control (which should rather be called population stabilization) number of 2 children per family is just an average. It does not mean that each and every family was compelled to have exactly 2 children. That would be a hard thing to do, and very inefficient. Remember that efficiency is one of the 144,000 attributes of God.

3. What it means is that when you consider the entire population and count all the children, they average 2 children per family. There are families

that will have as few as 1 child, or no children at all, while some families will have as many as 12 (I have not seen a situation where a family had more than 12 children, but it is possible that it could have happened because obviously I am not aware of all the situations in the entire period of our history of 78 trillion years).

4. Now even if it did happen, it will not change the average, because of the following reason:

5. Their custom is that when married couples start to have children, the Chiefs and Judges are involved in the family planning of each and every couple, because they are responsible for population stabilization.

6. They are the ones who will give certain families permission to have more than 2 children after they have consulted with other couples in the town to find out which among them plan to have no children at all in their present incarnation, and how many plan to have only 1 child.

7. Such plans are always finalized in advance by each family, according to the details of their destiny; in other words, what is their mission on earth in that particular incarnation, and what will

be their contribution to their town, their clan, their Tribe and the Nation as a whole.

8. As soon as the Judges have a complete idea of each family's plan, as to how many are to have 1 child or no children at all, then they inform the Chiefs, who are then afforded the leeway to give permission to those parents who want a large family, up to as many as 12 children, as I said before.

9. When the Judges take a population census, as they do periodically, they will know how far below the total their town is, and so some other town will then have the opportunity to make up for the deficit by allowing those parents who have expressed a desire to have 3, 4, 5 or more children to go ahead and do so.

10. So the total number of children in a given census period may be below average in some towns, and above average in others, but the total will always be adjusted so that the average of 2 children per family is reached, thereby ensuring that the planet in every millennium, has its maximum of 1B8M people.

11. Considering that we are talking about very long-lived people, the next obvious question now is, when do they actually have children, and how often. Do they have children like modern people do, meaning that at all times there are children born somewhere on earth, or do they use a different and more natural method appropriate for long-lived beings.

12. The answer is that they do not have children at all times like modern people do. Our modern method is very unnatural, being forced on us by the fact that we live a very short life.
Their custom of child-bearing was as follows:

13. It was determined a long time ago, at the very beginning (by the Original People on the first earth) that the best way for children to be raised and educated properly, is when as many children as possible are around at the same time.

14. So they have a law which states that parents may bear children only during the period that is set aside as the child-bearing period. This is a period that is about 100 years long, give or take several years, and it occurs only once every 1,000 years. Once that period is over, parents are not allowed to

have any more children until the next 100-year period comes around, one thousand years later.

15. The law states very explicitly that any child that would be born after the child-bearing period is over, such a child will be taken by the Judges and sent back to the ancestral world. Let me state here that I have been told that in all the history of our Nation, such a thing has never happened. Every person on earth knows the law, and it has never been contravened even once in all of our 78 trillion-year history.

16. Anyone who thinks that this is impossible does not have a good understanding of our ancient ways. Our laws were not laws as laws are known today, but were actually customs based on nature, and meant to enhance the lives of the ancients. Any person who would go against the laws would be going against their own desires and self-interest.

17. The people actually loved their laws (customs) because they saw clearly how their lives were enhanced by such laws, resulting in greater happiness, peace and spiritual advancement.

18. Normally, most if not all of the childless couples who wish to have children will have all their

children during their first 100-year period of child-bearing. It does happen that some parents will have their first children during the first 100-year period, then have more during the second 100-year period, a thousand years later.

19. But this is very rare. The common way is to have all their children during their first 100-year period of child-bearing, so that all the siblings in the family will be separated by just a few years, as is the case even today.

20. Taking into account the full 100-year period, it stands to reason that the oldest children of that generation will be only about 100 years older than the youngest - no more than 100 years.

21. This turns out to be a very good and practical way to ensure that the whole generation, which amounts to about 144,000,000 youths, will be able to attend the education rituals at about the same time, and more importantly, be able to attend the first Great Ritual of the Black Nation together, all 144 million of them at the same time.

22. With this customary practice, as you can imagine, most of the time on earth there will be no children to be found anywhere. And by children I

mean those cute little ones 10 years old and under that are always running around and playing tirelessly and providing a lot of pleasure to adults. Such children are around for only about 100 years and then that's it.

23. They are nowhere to be seen after that for the next 900 years, until the next child-rearing period comes around 1,000 years later. Remember that even though the people live to be 7,000 years old or more, their childhood period is exactly like ours today, it ends when they are about 10,11,12,13, or 14 years old.

24. Therefore every 1,000 years the entire Nation, especially women, look forward to this 100-year child-bearing period. It is a time of joy and great happiness like no other. The entire planet practically comes to a stop during the child-bearing period. The following 900 years or so, after all the children of that generation have been born and have grown up, there are no little ones to be found anywhere on the entire planet.

25. Every person, starting with the childless couples (who will be parents soon), on to their parents (who will be grandparents), and then the great-grandparents, then the great-great-grandparents,

then the gr-gr-gr-grandparents, then the gr-gr-gr-gr-grandparents, and lastly (but not least) the 7,000-year old gr-gr-gr-gr-gr-grandparents or senior citizens who are about to ascend, but will not do so until they have enjoyed that 100 years with their gr-gr-gr-gr-gr-grandchildren - every one of them is in a state of unbounded joy brought about by the presence of children. It is quite an amazing spectacle to behold, this child-rearing period.

26. To be honest with you, I was very saddened the first time I became aware of it. Seeing all the children grown up with no little ones running around anywhere on the entire planet really saddened me - to think that the people will not see children for a whole 900 years!

27. But it was explained to me that my sadness was brought about by the fact that our lives today are so short. This fact was interfering with my thought process, causing me to think that I personally would never see children there again because of my short life-span.

28. The ancients themselves are not bothered by this at all. I came to realize that on the contrary, this absence of children for 900 years is part of the reason why their joy is so unbounded when children

are present. Perhaps if they were always in the presence of children like we are today, their joy would be tempered somewhat.

29. The 7,000-year old citizens spend a lot of time with the children during these last years of their lives on earth. They will see them pass through puberty and go through all their ritual education until they reach the age of 77 years old and become full citizens of the earth when they complete the perfection of their character and get ready to contribute their unique talents to society. Only after that do the senior citizens decide that it is now time to ascend.

30. When they do, it is a long-standing tradition that those very same children, who are now full adults, will have the front row seat in the arena at the ascension ceremony of their patriarch and matriarch, their oldest living relatives. The oldest boy and girl (really man and woman) among all the gr-gr-gr-gr-gr-grandchildren will be the ones who hold the hands of the patriarch and matriarch as they get ready to ascend.

5

Re-populating The

Earth

There are several possible scenarios of how the 144,000 will increase the population of perfect people to the final number of 1B8M.

2. The future is not known definitely except by the 24 Elders, but it's not difficult to see that one of several scenarios will happen. One such scenario is as follows:

3. Initially there will be a few people among the 144,000 elect who are on earth right now who will be the first to resurrect (while still living) into the perfect ancient bodies that are in the pyramid temple. Then soon after that we may see the

appearance of the anti-christ followed by the appearance of the extra-terrestrials to perform their rapture scheme.

4. That will be followed by the arrival of Yahweh who will rule the earth from that point on until the end of the 7,000 year period of the existence of the non-blacks.

5. By then, there will be 12 major communities of Black people who will be living all over the world. The communities will vary in size. Some will have about 14,000 people, which is the minimum necessary to form a town or city. Others will have many, many more, upwards of 100,000 people all living together and supporting one another.

6. Regardless of the size of the communities, each one will have a core of 12,000 people who are part of the 144,000. These 12,000 in each one of the 12 communities will be surrounded by people who are not part of the 144,000, but who will be glad to be helping the core to rebuild the society of the Black Nation.

7. There will not be any jealousies or envy about being or not being part of the 144,000, as people by then will be aware of the mission of the 144,000,

which is to re-populate the earth with the new types of people.

8. They will be aware that even though they will not be physically resurrected into those ancient bodies like the 144,000 elect, they nevertheless will incarnate into those bodies after they pass on and when new people are born. And so they will do all that is required of them to facilitate the mission of the 144,000.

9. The organization of these communities of self-reliant Black people began some decades ago, and will continue through the year 2012 and beyond, until the total number of the elect reaches the minimum of 144,000. So when the major events and appearances outlined above take place, even though the majority of Black people will still be for the most part in a state of self-forgetfulness, the 144,000 on the other hand will be mentally wide awake and socially and economically separated from the world of the light races.

10. It is expected that four of these communities will be located in the United States, in the south, east, central and western parts of the country.

11. In addition to the four in the US, there will be two more; one in South America (most likely Brazil), and another one in the islands, either Haiti or Jamaica. That will make a total of 6 communities in the west.

12. There will be four in Africa, one in Israel and one in India. These communities will begin to have the ancient languages and customs resurrected in their minds. The major catalyst for their cultural re-awakening will be the resurrected Judges mentioned before, who will travel all over the world to these communities and initiate them into the ancient languages, as well as the culture and science.

13. The initiation of the rest of the 144,000 will begin prior to the arrival of Yahweh. That will prepare them to help as many Black people as possible to get through the trying times that are soon to come with the appearance of the anti-christ.

2. As the rest of the 144,000 approach the time of their own physical resurrection, they will apply the ancient sciences to prepare their lands. They will produce new plants and animals, and make dramatic transformations to the lands they live on.

3. Soon thereafter, when their lands are ready and their new animals and plants have increased, the rest of them will begin to undergo physical, conscious resurrection while still living in their present bodies, and continue to do so until the number of Judges reaches the total of 144,000.

14. At that point when all 144,000 are resurrected and present on earth (having been joined by the ancients who resurrected in the old days, such as the mahdis and all their soul mates) then they will be in a position to work more effectively in soul mate pairs. Each Judge of the newly resurrected will find his or her soul mate. They will begin to have children in order to start re-populating the earth with perfect people.

15. Of the several possible scenarios as to how the population numbers will increase, I will choose one that I think is most likely. As I stated before, only the Elders know the future in all its details, and know how the re-population process will unfold. But whichever scenario will come about, the end result will be the same.

16. So the particular scenario itself is not the critical thing, but rather the fact that when the year 2914 comes around, exactly 7,000 years since the full

appearance of the non-black races, the entire Black population will again have regained their natural, perfect bodies which we had lost in order to experience this cycle, which is winding down to an end:

17. - Year 2050 will see all 144,000 resurrected in perfect bodies, being the Judges.

18. The 144,000 (72,000 soul mates) will give birth to an average of 4 children per family over a 6 to 10 year period, until around the year 2060. So the total number of children in perfect bodies in the year 2060 will be:

72,000 families x 4 children per family = 288,000 children

19. (Note: Again, the 4 children-per-family number does not mean that each and every family will have exactly 4 children. That is unnatural and I would even go so far as to say it would be an impossible thing to orchestrate.

20. What it means is that when all the children are counted, their number will be about 288,000, and since there are 144,000 Judges (or 72,000 married

couples), then that averages to 4 children per family.

21. In reality some families will have only 1 child, while others will have 3,4,6 etc depending on their destiny. So if one were to take a census in 2060 and count all the children and families, their numbers would yield that average of 4 children per family.)

22. - Year 2060: The total population in perfect bodies (not counting the Elders and Chiefs) will approximately be:

288,000 children + 144,000 Judges = 432,000 people.

23. After about 20 years, around the year 2080, when the children have grown and found their soul mates, making 144,000 couples, they too will give birth to 4 children per family, say over a period of 10 years. The number of children will be: 144,000 couples x 4 children per couple = 576,000 children.

---

24. - Year 2090:

576,000 children
+ 288,000 parents
+ 144,000 Judges (grandparents)
_____

= 1,008,000 (1 million eight thousand people)

25. The 576,000 children (288,000 couples) will have 4 children each at about 20 years of age, around the year 2110 through 2120.
That is 288,000 couples x 4 children per family = 1,152,000 children

_____

26. - Year 2120:

1,152,000 children
+ 576,000 parents
+ 288,000 grandparents
+ 144,000 Judges (great-grandparents)
_____

= 2,160,000 people

27. The 1,152,000 children (576,000 couples) will have 4 children each at about 20 years of age, around the year 2140 through 2150.

That is 576,000 couples x 4 children per family = 2,304,000 children

28. - Year 2150:

    2,304,000 children
+ 1,152,000 parents
+   576,000 grandparents
+   288,000 great-grandparents
+   144,000 Judges (great-great-grandparents)
_____
= 4,464,000 people

29. The 2,304,000 children (1,152,000 couples) will have 4 children each at about 20 years of age, around the year 2170 through 2180.

That is 1,152,000 couples x 4 children per family = 4,608,000 children

_____

30. - Year 2180:

    4,608,000 children
+ 2,304,000 parents
+ 1,152,000 grandparents
+   576,000 great-grandparents
+   288,000 gr-gr-grandparents
+   144,000 Judges (gr-gr-gr-grandparents)
_____
= 9,072,000 people

31. The 4,608,000 children (2,304,000 couples) will have 4 children each at about 20 years of age, around the year 2200 through 2210.

That is 2,304,000 couples x 4 children per family = 9,216,000 children

---

32. - Year 2210:

    9,216,000 children
+   4,608,000 parents
+   2,304,000 grandparents
+   1,152,000 great-grandparents
+   576,000 gr-gr-grandparents
+   288,000 gr-gr-gr-grandparents
+   144,000 Judges (gr-gr-gr-gr-grandparents)

= 18,288,000 people

33. The 9,216,000 children (4,608,000 couples) will have 4 children each at about 20 years of age, around the year 2230 through 2240.

That is 4,608,000 couples x 4 children per family = 18,432,000 children

---

34.   - Year 2240:

    18,432,000 children
+   9,216,000 parents
+   4,608,000 grandparents
+   2,304,000 great-grandparents
+   1,152,000 gr-gr-grandparents
+   576,000 gr-gr-gr-grandparents
+   288,000 gr-gr-gr-gr-grandparents
+   144,000 Judges (gr-gr-gr-gr-gr-grandparents)
_____

=   36,720,000 people

35.   The 18,432,000 children (9,216,000 couples) will have 4 children each at about 20 years of age, around the year 2260 through 2270.
That is 9,216,000 couples x 4 children per family = 36,864,000 children

_____

36.   - Year 2270:

    36,864,000 children
+   18,432,000 parents
+   9,216,000 grandparents
+   4,608,000 great-grandparents
+   2,304,000 gr-gr-grandparents
+   1,152,000 gr-gr-gr-grandparents
+   576,000 gr-gr-gr-gr-grandparents
+   288,000 gr-gr-gr-gr-gr-grandparents
+   144,000 Judges (gr-gr-gr-gr-gr-gr-grandparents)
_____

=   73,584,000 people

37. At this point the population is approaching 144,000,000 people.

The Judges decide that the average number of children per family will be reduced from 4 to about 3.8 per family, so around the years 2290 to 2300 the number born will be:

8,432,000 couples x approx. 3.8 children per couple = 70,416,000 children

38. - Year 2300:

      70,416,000 children
+   36,864,000 parents
+   18,432,000 grandparents
+   9,216,000 great-grandparents
+   4,608,000 gr-gr-grandparents
+   2,304,000 gr-gr-gr-grandparents
+   1,152,000 gr-gr-gr-gr-grandparents
+   576,000 gr-gr-gr-gr-gr-grandparents
+   288,000 gr-gr-gr-gr-gr-gr-grandparents
+   144,000 Judges (gr-gr-gr-gr-gr-gr-gr-grandparents)
      _____
=   144,000,000 people

39. The Judges at this point have been resurrected for more than 250 years, and their oldest children are about 250 years old.

A few Black people are still incarnating in these modern bodies we have now because there are not yet enough ancient-type bodies.

40. Now the average number of children per family is reduced again to its final and permanent level of 2 children per family.

- Year 2300: the population is 144 million (144M)
- Years 2320-2330: the population doubles to 2x144M=288M
- Years 2350-2360: the population triples to 3x144M=432M
- Years 2380-2390: the population is four-fold, 4x144M=576M
- Years 2410-2420: the population is five-fold, 5x144M=720M
- Years 2440-2450: the population is six-fold, 6x144M=864M
- Years 2470-2480: the population is seven-fold, 7x144M=1B8M

41. So around the year 2480 the population reaches its maximum of 1B8M. The world of the modern-type body Black people will then come to an end as all Black people will now be incarnated in the ancient type bodies. Only the non-blacks will be left under Yahweh's rule.

42. At that time, the Judges have been resurrected now for over 430 years, and their oldest children are about 430 years old. The Judges are gr-gr-gr-gr-gr-gr-gr-gr-gr-gr-gr-gr-gr-grandparents. In other words, there are 16 generations of perfect people living at the same time on earth.

43. The Judges have completed their mission of ushering in the full population of 1B8M perfect people, and have been alive for over 430 years since their resurrection, in addition to the thousands of years they lived before they laid down their bodies. Remember that the Judges are full Gods. They completed the 7 great rituals of the Black Nation long, long ago, long before they laid down their bodies in the Temple of Resurrection.

44. During these 430+ years of re-populating the earth, they will be teaching and leading the people as full Gods. That is what the physical resurrection of the 144,000 so-called elect really means. It means to resurrect from being a man to being a God. When they resurrect, they will recognize that they are full Gods.

45. Many people who will still be in our present types of bodies will see living Gods in the flesh walking on earth. There will literally be two

different worlds existing side by side; the world of ordinary people with present-type bodies, who will be decreasing in number, who will be ruled by Yahweh until the year 2914.

46. They will be living right next to the world of Gods increasing in number, led by the 144,000 Judges. They will lead, teach, and initiate people as full Gods, as they used to do in their ancient perfect society.

6

TIME TRAVEL

B rother Blackroots,

2. Thanks for the reply. On the same question, was the dream given the person by his higher self? do yuou think we can all see the future in a dream or do you know any ritual to access the future ?

3. Yes the dream was a vision given to the person by his Higher Self, and no, there is no ritual to enable a person to access the future.

4. We have rituals for sending people to the past using our system of Ditoro as I have already

explained in the book. But there are no rituals for sending them to the future.

5. The reason is simply because the future has not happened yet. We can investigate the past in order to gain knowledge that we can use in the present so that we can have the wisdom to advance into the future with balance and harmony. That's really the reason why we go back in time to the past. As far as the future is concerned, only God (the 24 Elders) knows the future.

6. We write our future when we are united with the minds of the Elders before we incarnate. After our incarnation, our conscious memory starts as a blank slate. We no longer have knowledge of the future. This is an essential part of our lives, that we should start from a blank slate.

7. That makes our lives original and genuine. Everything that happens is brand new to us, and we react to it in a genuine way. If we knew all the details of our future, then our lives would lose that genuineness and originality.

8. Now, it's possible – and it does happen a lot – that certain events in our future are shown to us. This always happens in a spontaneous way, meaning

it is never initiated or controlled by the person, only by the Higher Self.

9. Such visions can occur when a person is wide awake or asleep in a dream. When such visions occur, it is because the Higher Self wants the person to have that particular information for reasons that are known only to the Higher Self.

10. Such visions happened many times to the prophets of old. They still happen today to many people. When they do, it is always the Higher Self showing the person part of the future. It is not possible for the person to use any type of ritual to access those visions or any part of the future by themselves.

11. Of course it's possible for other beings to show people visions and mislead them into thinking those are real visions of the future. This has to do with the abuse of the psychic power. There are those, especially extra-terrestrials, who are very adept at this type of thing.

12. They take advantage of the fact that most people really live in a state of sleeping wakefulness. They are able to put all kinds of visions in the minds

of some people and convince them that they see the future.

13. When you read stories of extra-terrestrial contact with humans, and all the predictions that these extra-terrestrials made in the past, you will not find one that has ever come true, and yet people continue to be misled. So how can one tell the difference between genuine visions and deceitful ones?

14. The Higher Self gives visions only to people who know his/her 'voice'. Just like it says in the bible, the sheep know the voice of their shepherd, and can never be misled by the voice of another. They listen only to their shepherd and no one else.

15. The way to know the voice of your Higher Self is to practice listening to it. With enough practice, you will be able to recognize it because it is unique, unlike any other type of communication that can enter your mind. That is why it is so important to do the exercises in the 2nd level of Blackroots Science as given in the book.

16. By practicing consistently, you will reach a point where you recognize the voice of your Higher Self so well that no one can deceive you. At that point you

will begin to receive visions from the Higher Self and know that they are true.

17. In the case of going to the past, of course this can be done by using rituals, because the past is our history. All nations must study their history to know themselves and to gain wisdom. Modern people do it by reading books or making films of their history.

18. That is part of their system of education. Our system of education uses the ritual method to study history, as well as the story-telling done by elders and griots and so on. So the past is an open book because it has already happened.

19. Anyone with the ability to do so can access any part of it. Accessing it is simply part of our education, exactly like listening to your grandparents tell you about their lives before you were born.

20. Not so with the future. The future is sacred knowledge available only to Modimo, the Most High One. For all other people, it is not possible to go there and investigate it like we do with the past. So there are no rituals designed for doing that.

21. Now, there are people who like to claim that they have seen people come from the future, or that they themselves can go to the future. How can you go to a place that does not yet exist? And how can people be living in and coming back from a place that does not exist?

22. All such ideas are fanciful imaginations or fabrications used to serve some nefarious purpose that has nothing to do with the truth. The future can be predicted to some extent using logical analysis based on events of the past and present, and being able to see trends.

23. For example, as you know, weather can be predicted reasonably accurately for short intervals by studying weather patterns. Similarly technological advancement can also be predicted for short intervals by studying trends, the same with many other phenomena like social trends, biological trends and so on.

24. Beyond those short intervals there are just too many variables that make it impossible to predict with reliable accuracy, not to mention the effect that the unknown plans of the Elders have on the future, which can change the future in directions that no one can ever predict.

25. So when some people say they have been to the future, if they are not telling outright lies, then what they are doing is using their imagination to try and predict what the future will look like.

26. People with very active imaginations and exceptional abilities to visualize can 'see' those future predictions so clearly that they see themselves actually there, living in and observing the 'future'.

27. But regardless of how clearly they see that, it is nothing but their imaginations. It does not in any way mean that those futures they see actually exist. They simply do not because the future has not happened yet.

28. The only scenarios of the future that are 'set in stone', so to speak, are those that the Most High shows the person in a vision. Those are part of what is already written because they are part of the plan of the Elders, who are the only ones who know the future in all its details.

29. As far as people coming back from the future, that is also impossible because the future has not been experienced yet. The Most High uses the present, the NOW moment, to experience what He

knows, then that NOW moment becomes the past, and becomes available for us to learn from it.

30. So God, in the bodies of people, experiences it, then makes it available for us to see and gain wisdom from it. We cannot see His experiences before He experiences them.

31. Wisdom is directly linked to experience of the truth. Without experiencing the truth, there is no wisdom that can be gained – and there is certainly no wisdom that can be gained from experiencing fanciful imaginations.

7

THE 7 GREAT RITUALS

Our universe is still increasing in size as more star systems are being created from the center of the universe.

2. When the universe is complete, it will have over 125 bil tr tr star systems. The suns of these star systems, such as our sun, are called first tier suns.

3. The star systems are created in groups that modern people call galaxies. Each galaxy on average has over 177 trillion stars.

4. At the center of each galaxy is a large sun called a second tier sun around which the stars of the galaxy revolve. The second tier suns of most

galaxies are still in the first stage of materialization called magnetism. Only the oldest galaxies close to the center of the universe have suns that have fully materialized through the stages of magnetism, electricity, light and ether, and appear as giant orbs of light.

5. After the completion of the universe, there will be over 700 million trillion galaxies. All these galaxies are created in groups of 10,000. The 10,000 galaxies in the group revolve around an even larger sun called a third tier sun. There are over 70,000 trillion groups of 10,000 - and therefore there are over 70,000 tr third tier suns.

6. These 70,000 tr groups are further sub-divided into groups of 10,000. There are 7 trillion of these groups, each group revolving around a fourth tier sun. Therefore there are 7 tr fourth tier suns.

7. The 7 tr fourth tier groups are further sub-divided into groups of 14,000, each group revolving around a fifth tier sun. There are exactly 504 million of these groups, and therefore there are 504 million fifth tier suns.

8. These 504 million suns are further sub-divided into 12 groups. Each group has 42 million fifth tier

suns revolving around a sixth tier sun; therefore there are 12 sixth tier suns.

9. The 12 sixth tier suns revolve around one seventh tier sun, which is the largest and first sun created. It is located at the center of the universe.

10. The 7th tier sun is the location of what is called heaven, the original abode of the 1B8M Gods. The 12 sixth tier suns revolving around it comprise what are called the 12 pearly gates of heaven. The 7th sun, the location of 'heaven', can only be entered through one of these 'gates', or sixth tier suns.

11. Each sixth tier sun is the center of a 'universe'. Although the universe is one, it is nonetheless divided into 12 parts, each part being, as it were, a complete, self-contained universe. All these 12 'universes' are equal in size, and are located equidistant around the central or universal sun.

12. They are located - or rather will be located (at the end of the universe) - around the central sun in the form of what modern mathematicians call a dodecahedron.

13. That means they will be located equidistant all around the sphere of the central sun, and they will

revolve around it in orbital circuits that are perfectly aligned to do so in a perfect and harmonious way.

14. At the end, when the universe has reached a complete, perfect state, it is used as the first earth of the next creation. The universe at that point will be a spherical orb. The central sun of the universe will then become the central sun of that first earth, located right at its core.

15. The 12 sixth tier suns revolving around this central core will be re-arranged in such a way that they are equidistantly placed around the core or central sun, as mentioned before. These 12 suns will become the 12 primary nodes of the first earth.

16. Hence every orb created in the new universe after that will be patterned after the first earth, meaning that they will all have 12 primary nodes - this includes all orbs, whether they are planets or suns.

17. Each one of these 12 suns (which become primary nodes) are surrounded by 42 million fifth tier suns, as already mentioned. When a planet becomes ready for habitation, the 12 nodes become

the center of each of the 12 countries belonging to the 12 Tribes.

18. The 42 million fifth tier suns are the secondary nodes around each one of the 12 primary nodes. The 12 primary nodes represent the 12 Gods who will rule the earth, manifested in the flesh as 24 Elders; 12 men and 12 women - soul mates.

19. The 42 million secondary nodes represent the 42 million Gods who will become the citizens of each country, incarnating in the flesh as 84 million people; 42 million men and 42 million women - soul mate couples. The pattern is repeated 12 times in the 12 countries, the location of each country being determined by the primary nodes.

20. As the planet gets older and becomes more and more stable, and as the continents are re-arranged repeatedly over the ages, the nodes move around as well, establishing new locations for the capital of each country according to the orders of the Elders, executed by the Chiefs.

21. Now, there are seven Great Rituals in the education system of the Black Nation. The seven Rituals correspond directly to the seven tiers of suns in the universe.

22. People take part in the first Great Ritual when they reach the age of about 1,000 years. Then they engage in one Ritual every 1,000 years after that, until they complete all seven, the last one being when they are about 7,000 years of age.

23. After they complete the first Great Ritual, they gain the power that resides in the sun, such as ours, called a first tier sun. The power of the sun encompasses our entire solar system and beyond, all the way to the boundary with the other nearby sun systems.

24. Thus these initiates are called 'first tier' initiates, for lack of a better word. They gain knowledge, understanding and power over all that exists within our solar system right up to the boundary. That means they know the vibrational 'name' or image and nature of every thing that exists in our solar system.

25. They remain at this stage of power for 1,000 years. During that time, they 'consolidate' that power within themselves, making it a part of themselves in every conceivable way. The 'consolidation' takes a thousand years, and cannot be completed any sooner because of the natural

laws inherent in the ritual process, in the way it affects the body and mind.

26. The 'consolidation' of power includes not only power over our solar system, but over any solar system in the galaxy, one at a time. This means whichever sun system they may happen to visit, they have the same power over it as they have in this solar system.

27. Once they have done that, after 1,000 years, they are then ready to take part in the second Great Ritual. The second Great Ritual gives them galactic-sun power, or the power of the 2nd tier sun, and they become 2nd tier initiates. Similarly it takes 1,000 years to 'consolidate' 2nd tier power.

28. Even though the galaxy is that much bigger than the solar system, it still takes only 1,000 years because their ability to consolidate increases with every higher Ritual.

29. After another 1,000 years they complete the 3rd Great Ritual and gain the power of the 3rd tier sun, which is the sun of 10,000 galaxies. Then they spend 1,000 years to have that power totally inculcated in them.

30. The 4th Great Ritual gives them the power of the 4th tier sun, which is the sun of over 100 million galaxies

31. The 5th Great Ritual gives them all the power of the 5th tier sun, which is the nourisher of over 1 trillion galaxies.

32. After completing the 6th Great Ritual, they gain the power of the 6th tier sun, which is the overseer of over 58 million trillion galaxies.

33. Then finally they complete the 7th Great Ritual, which endows them with the power of the universal sun, the sun of 700 million trillion galaxies. When they reach this stage, they become citizens of the universe. They become citizens of the first earth which is located at the center of the universe, at the core of the universal sun.

34. The inhabitants of the first earth live on that planet inside the universal sun, surrounded by its golden atmosphere. The golden atmosphere inside each sun is the repository of all things over which the sun has guardianship. Since the universal sun has guardianship over the entire universe, it is the 'repository', so to speak, of all that exists in the universe.

35. That means everything that exists in our galaxy can be accessed inside our galactic sun; and everything that exists in the universe, can be accessed in the golden atmosphere of the universal sun. There is a reason why the golden and silvery colors are used, and that is because they are superior to all other colors in recording and reproducing without any loss.

36. The inhabitants of the first earth use the universal sun to interact with and travel to any part of the universe. They can see any part of the universe from inside the universal sun. When they want to contact someone or travel to some place in the universe, they first 'summon' the 6th tier sun of that location.

37. The sun will appear before them. It actually appears in the mind's eye, but their imagination is so strong that the image actually materializes as a light orb in front of them. Then they 'step' right into it and are instantly at that place where that sun is located.

38. When they are there, inside the 6th tier sun, they 'summon' the 5th tier sun of their desired location, and it too appears before them, and by

'stepping' into it they transport themselves instantly to its location.

39. By using the word 'summon', I am trying to convey an idea that is somewhat similar to the summoning of a taxi cab. You wait at the street and call a taxi on your phone. It drives up and stops before you, you enter it and it transports you to your desired location.

40. The de-materialization process is somewhat analogous. They start by standing at the designated location inside the 6th tier sun. Then using the mind, they 'call' the 5th tier sun by its vibrational name, or visualizing it as it is, and it instantly appears before them as a golden or sometimes silvery light orb, about the size of twice the height of a person.

41. Then they step right into it and find themselves instantly inside that 5th tier sun, trillions of light years away, wherever that sun is actually located. Then they repeat the process and move many more light years to the 4th tier sun, then to the 3rd and finally to the 2nd, or the central sun of the galaxy they wish to visit.

42. Once they are inside the galactic sun, they can summon any star in that galaxy, for example our sun. Then they find themselves inside our sun, and then have access to any planet or place in our solar system.

43. To visit their host on earth, they simply 'summon' his location, which could be a room in his house, which will immediately appear before them, and they simply step into it and are instantly inside the actual room in the house of their host on earth. So just like that they can move from any part of the universe to anywhere else instantly. The distance makes no difference to how quick they get there.

44. The step-by-step process I have described may give the impression that it actually takes a noticeable amount of time to move from sun to sun and eventually to the final location.

45. In actual practice, it takes a fraction of a second, because what they actually do is 'summon' all the destinations simultaneously in their minds, and thus they move through all of them at the speed of thought, which makes it appear as if they moved from point A to point D without stopping at B and C.

46. That is not so. They just move as fast as their minds are able to simultaneously 'call' on the various stopping places in-between, and finally find themselves at the final location. They only stop at the intermediate locations for longer if they have the need to do so.

47. To travel back from the earth, they use one of the many secondary nodal points that exist on earth. As mentioned before, there are 42 million of them in every country, although not all of them are easily accessible.

48. They act as portals between our earth and other nearby planets, as well as to the sun itself, which is the main portal for going to the center of the galaxy. These portals are actually located many miles inside the earth.

49. They 'fan' outward in the form of a cone, all the way to many miles above the earth. Hence they can be accessed just as easily above the earth in space as they can on the surface of the earth. When they are used by people, they are accesses on the surface, and when used by interplanetary spacecraft, they are accessed in space above the earth.

50. The de-materialization of objects uses the same principle of 'summoning'. To bring an object to themselves, they 'call' its real name, which is the same as visualizing it as it really is, and it appears before their mind's eye. As soon as they release it, it materializes before them.

51. Thus the Great Rituals grace them with the power to know every single thing in the universe, and to be able to summon it by its real name, which is its true image or vibration, and to enter its location if it's a place, or move it to themselves or to another place if it's a smaller object.

52. Those are some of the powers inherent in the Great Rituals. There are many more, but it's not necessary to mention them. The ones mentioned are enough to give an idea of their glory.

53. **if there are millions of portals, how come we dont see people disapear in and out of them everyday?**

54. The portals are always closed. To go through, one has to open it first.

55. **Can u open a portal?**

56. No, at the level of my training I am unable to open a portal by myself.

57. **Can u open it with the help of someone ?**

58. Yes, I am able to open it with my soul mate.

59. **Wooow! can u tell me where the portals are?**

60. There are thousands of them right here in California

61. **Where exactly?**

62. There is one inside the house where I live here in California. That is how me and my wife travel to and from our village.

8

DESCRIPTION OF THE
ANCIENTS

G reetings Brother,

2. As promised, here is a short description of the ancients. I'm not going to go into too much detail for reasons that I already made clear to you.

3. The ancients, compared to modern people, age like us until they reach the age of about 16 years, then they age about 1 year every 500 years, until they look about 28, then they completely stop aging.

4. A young person of 16 years will remain looking like a 16 year-old until he/she reaches the age of about 500 years old. When they are between the ages of 500 and 1,000 years, they look like they are 17 years old.

1,000 to 1,500 - look like 18 years old.
1,500 to 2,000 - look like 19 years old.
2,000 to 2,500 - look like 20 years old.
2,500 to 3,000 - look like 21 years old.
3,000 to 3,500 - look like 22 years old.
3,500 to 4,000 - look like 23 years old.
4,000 to 4,500 - look like 24 years old.
4,500 to 5,000 - look like 25 years old.
5,000 to 5,500 - look like 26 years old.
5,500 to 6,000 - look like 27 years old.
6,000 to 7,000 - look like they are 28 years old, and remain that way forever.

5. Their skin is so smooth it looks like they have no pores. They actually do have pores, but they are very small, so much so that at first glance you will think they don't have them. The skin is very deep black; in texture it reminds me of the toner in a laser printer.

6. But they do have different hues to their skin. The hues are not so easy to see the first time, but after a while you can see clearly that they have

seven basic hues, and other mixed hues that occur when they inter-marry, as I will explain later.

7.   The hues of their blackness correspond to the seven basic colors. They have a reddish black, an orangish black, a yellowish black, a greenish black, a blue-black, an indigo-black, and a violet-black hue.

8.   These hues are not according to tribe, as one might think at first glance. They are found in all the Tribes. Most of the time people of the same hue will marry one another, regardless of which Tribe they belong to. But occasionally it does happen that soul mates can be of a different hue.

9.   When this happens, it results in children that have what can be clearly seen, upon close inspection, as a mixed hue of black, meaning they could be a mix of, say, reddish-black and greenish-black, giving them a hue somewhat between the two.

10.   Such occurrences are very few in number. The vast majority of soul mates are of the same hue of blackness, and the seven basic hues are for the most part predominant throughout the entire Nation.

11. The eye is pitch-black, all the same in all people. It is a black that is even deeper than their skin blackness. When you stare deep into the blackness of their eye, it is like looking into infinity.

12. The small central part is even blacker than the rest of the eye! The surrounding part is pure white, making their eyes the most beautiful part of their body. Their perfect, even teeth are the same pure white color.

13. Their hair is the most extraordinary thing about their physical appearance. It is black in youth, and remains so even in senior citizens. But I was told that it turns snow-white with extreme old age; that is, when they get to be around 100,000 years old, as with the Chiefs and the Elders.

14. The hair can be either curly or straight according to their will. I mean that literally. They are able to uncurl or curl their hair simply by their own will. When it is tightly curled, it is no more than about a quarter inch to a half-inch long. But when fully uncurled, it becomes straight and will hang down a long way, past the shoulders.

15. It is very fascinating, to put it mildly, when one sees their hair, looking very, very short in extremely

tight curls, unwind until it is perfectly straight and reaches all the way to the waist in some women.

16. As to why they sometimes have it in tight curls and other times hanging down straight, has to do with their activities that require the hair to be in one condition or the other. This is quite natural for them; their hair will curl or uncurl spontaneously without much thought from them, although they can make it do so at will.

17. Now, fifty thousand years ago when we left civilization and went into the forests of Africa, we lost our natural ability to control our hair like the ancients. The conditions we were living in forced our hair to remain in tight curls all the time.

18. This was necessary because during that time we lived dangerously amid untamed animals that we no longer knew how to control with our minds. Added to that was the fact that we no longer engaged in rituals that would require our hair to hang loose and straight, so we never did straighten it from that time on.

19. The hair strand acts somewhat like a long muscle, although it is not a muscle - it reacts to an electrical impulse, as one can see when the arm

hair is raised by static electricity, or when a person is afraid and the neck hair stands up straight.

20. When it is forced to remain in one position for a long time, it will 'atrophy' in that position just like a muscle will do. And so after many millennia, the hair of those people who lived in forests on the African continent became permanently curled in tight spirals.

21. On other continents, it curled only slightly, such as can be seen among the Maori of Australia, who are the descendents of those who came from Lemuria. Others, especially on the American and Indian continents, experienced the exact opposite. They engaged in some rituals that only required their hair to remain in a straight position, and it stayed permanently straight.

22. When the time came for Yahweh and the Elohim to make the light races, among the 60,000 volunteers who went to the island of Pelan, the majority were the descendents of people whose physical changes happened on the African continent, and thus the majority had curly African hair.

23. About a third of them had either straight hair or loose curls, such as can be seen among the ancient Greeks. When the scientists bred the races, they wanted them to be as widely different as possible from the majority of Black people on the island, who, as mentioned, had mostly African curly hair - they wanted the races to be different in both their skin and hair.

24. So they selectively bred the light-skinned races not only according to skin color, but also according to hair texture. When the first race came out, they mostly came out with long loose curls. These are depicted quite accurately in the ancient Greek sculptures that can be seen even today.

25. When the second race came out, they had succeeded in breeding out all the curliness out of the hair, and thus the last three races all came out with straight hair. But many, many centuries down the line, there was inter-racial marriage between these races, especially between the original Greeks and the Caucasians, such that some Caucasians inherited the Greek curls, as can be seen even today.

26. On the other hand, the Black inhabitants of the island preferred curly African-type hair, and thus

the vast majority of purely Black people born on the island married mostly spouses who had that type of hair. When it became time for them to leave the island, there were almost none that any longer had straight hair.

27. And thus it is the situation today that the light-skinned races have straight hair and the Israelites, the descendents of the original Black people of Pelan, have curly African hair even though both the Israelites and the races came out of the same 60,000 ancestors.

28. Going back to my description of the ancients, their bodies, overall, are just too beautiful to describe. They are simply the pinnacle of perfection. There is not a single person who looks like he or she is overweight or underweight. They have the kinds of bodies that we can only dream about. Their beauty is so perfect it will make you cry!

29. Their bodies have a natural protection from birth. It consists of a magnetic field whose extension can be controlled from close to the skin to as much as 10 feet beyond the body. With certain initiates, it can even be extended as far as they wish, using their minds.

30. This magnetic field is not what people call an 'aura'. It is an actual physical field that can be seen plainly with the eyes, when it is given color. Starting from when they are children, it reacts instinctively to the surroundings.

31. When they reach the age of about 7 years old, they are able to control it to some extent. It has several functions. One of its functions is to protect the body against anything that could cause harm.

32. If you remember, I mentioned a while ago that with the ancients, there was no such thing as an 'accident' or premature death. This magnetic field is part of the reason why that is so.

33. If a person were to find himself in a situation that could cause harm to his body, then the magnetic field would extend instinctively to protect the body. Of course, such situations never occur in real life, because their lives are preordained, and 'accidents' are not part of their 'learning curve' as is the case with modern people.

34. But to explain how this field works, imagine that a person was busy at the construction of a large building, such as a Temple, being built with massive blocks of stone that weigh several tons.   And

imagine (theoretically) that an 'accident' happened where several of these massive blocks fell on the person, about to crush him to death.

35. If such a thing were to happen, then the magnetic field would naturally extend out a couple of feet all around the person to create an impenetrable shield (even if the person was fast asleep, because it is as instinctive as the hormones in our bodies).

36. The block of stone would bounce off the shield and not cause harm to the person. It doesn't matter how heavy the stone is, it would not be able to penetrate this natural shield, because magnetism is the 'hardest' physical substance in existence.

37. It would be like the stone hit an infinitely hard and immovable object, and will either crumble if it's a soft stone, or just fall to the side if it's a hard stone. Incredible as this function of the field is, it is actually not its main function. Its main function is to provide 'clothing' for people, and to keep their bodies clean. I will explain shortly what I mean.

38. First let me state another protective aspect. The field also protects their bodies against living organisms such as insects and animals. The people

have to do certain types of work or scientific research in forests where there are lots of untamed animals, especially insects, which are the most curious of all animals.

39. When they see people for the first time, they cannot resist the urge to get close to them. The people, when they enter the forest, will extend their protective field about ten feet beyond their bodies, so that no animal or insect can come within ten feet of them, except those that they allow to penetrate the field.

40. For example if there is a swarm of insects flying around nearby, and they want to look at only two of them, say a male and a female, then no other insects will be able to penetrate their shield except those two that they choose.

41. They have such perfect mental control over the mind of all animals that those two insects will find themselves being urged to come close, even land on their hand. If they wanted to, they could lie down in a forest full of wild animals and all kinds of insects and other micro-organisms, and no matter how curious they got, not a single one would get within 10 feet of the sleeping body.

42. They also place this magnetic field permanently in the openings of their houses where modern people would normally put doors and windows. To enter the house, they simply walk right through the field, but other things such as rain or dust, even animals, cannot enter.

43. Now, the main function of this field is to keep the body clean and to provide clothing (there is another function related to transportation, but only for a certain level of initiates). The ancients never ever have to take a bath. But of course they always do, being especially fond of swimming.

44. But this is not to clean their bodies; it is rather to interact with the water element for specific reasons, which I will not go into here. Their bodies are kept clean at all times by this same magnetic field, and this includes their teeth.

45. It acts as a natural sanitizer, removing excess fluids from their pores, as well as old skin that peels off, and removing anything that sticks to their skin from the outside as soon as they give the mental command. Thus their bodies are kept perfectly clean at all times.

46. In addition, when they grow to be about 7 years old, they are able to change the vibration of the field and give it colors.   That is how they make clothes for themselves.

47. Before the age of 7, the children just walk around naked or are 'dressed' by their parents, or older relatives, as the case may be, who do so by influencing the child's field.   But after 7, they are able to dress themselves by changing the colors of their own field.

48. All people (all things for that matter) have what is called an 'aura'.   This is an ultra-physical field of many colors that, today, can only be seen by those who train to see it.   In ancient times all people saw it naturally without any training.

49. When the ancients make clothes for themselves using the magnetic field, they make it correspond in colors as closely as possible to their aura.   Now, every person's aura is different.   The higher the initiate, the more spectacular is their aura, and the more intense are the colors.

50. During certain important functions, such as the higher rituals, the high initiates will duplicate the colors of their auras perfectly with their magnetic

field clothing. During such festivals, one can easily separate all the levels of initiation among the participants simply by looking at their clothes.

51. Now these are real clothes. They have been called garments of light by some that have seen them. They are intensely bright, and are what some in ancient literature have called 'raiments of light', as when John reported seeing Jesus with a white garment so bright that no fuller (bleaching) on earth could achieve that level of whiteness.

52. The making of colorful clothes in this age (as can be seen in the beautiful colorful apparel of the ancient Egyptians), using actual cloth, is but a feeble attempt to mimic the natural clothes of light worn by the ancients.

53. Watching them move, and watching the children play is quite something else. Imagine the elegance of a cheetah combined with the grace of a butterfly and the sure-footedness of a lion, and then multiply that a thousand times. That will give you some approximation of their graceful movements.

54. They have many, many games that they play - both adults and children. All their games are co-operative in nature. They never play games for the

sake of competition. To the uninitiated eye, some of their games may indeed seem like games of competition, but that is never the case.

55. For example, they have a game that is the equivalent of what we call a tug of war, played by adults. This is a mental game where two or more people will try to pull an object to themselves. You will see an object floating in the air between the contestants, both sides concentrating to pull the object to themselves.

56. Those with the stronger, more developed minds will always win. The aim of this game, especially when played between two people, is not to see who has the stronger mind. It's always clear that one of the contestants will have the stronger mind, being a higher initiate.

57. The aim of the game is to strengthen the minds of the other contestants. When they play this game, there is a whole lot of activity going on around the players, that they are forced to notice, sometimes even to take part in.

58. There are musicians playing music, women dancing, trained animals performing and many other activities that are hard to describe; all of whose aim

is to distract the players, thus forcing them to work even harder to concentrate.

59. A trainee will continue to take part in this game until a stale-mate is reached, where the object is suspended midway between the contestants, and neither one can move it.

60. At that point, the trainee has reached the same level of mental strength as the teacher, and will graduate from playing that particular game.

61. At another time I will attempt to describe some of their homes and towns without getting into too much detail, just to give you an idea of what their communal life was like.

9

BECOMING AN ELDER

b rotha, how do one become a Elder?

2. Becoming an Elder happens only by pre-ordination. The same is true for Chiefs and Judges as well. In the 78 trillion-year history of our planet, every single one of the B8M Gods has been an Elder at one time or another. In this reply I will talk about all 3 groups of our Leaders.

3. First of all, when I said a King or Queen rules for 25,000 years, that is only an estimate. They can rule anywhere from 25,000 to 35,000 years depending on their mission. The length of their reign is based on the cycle of the Sirius star which is 1,460 years.

4. The ruler rules for about 20 of these cycles, or 29,200 years; but they do not follow this cycle precisely - some will rule for a shorter period, some for a longer period, but the average is 29,200 years. The entire cycle for all 24 Elders to rule lasts for 24x29200 = 700800 years.

5. In our 78 tr-year history, there have been over 100 million of these cycles; so as you can imagine, each one of the B8M Gods has rotated into the Eldership at least twice - some twice and some three times.

6. When each and every one of the B8M has been an Elder 7 times, then our planet will reach a state of perfection. At that point new people will no longer be born on earth. When that time comes, we who will be on the planet as the last inhabitants, we will no longer ascend.

7. There will no longer be a governmental structure that rules the earth. All people will co-operate on the same high level like the Original People did on the first earth at the beginning of the universe.

8. This type of co-operation and co-ordination is instantaneous and perfect in every respect, as the people are all united as one in mind.

9. We will then live continuously while we help the rest of the younger planets that came after us, to join us in the state of perfection. These are planets to which we sent settlers from earth in the past. There are solar systems closer to the center of the universe that have already reached this state of perfection.

10. These are planets that long, long, ago, sent out settlers to occupy newly created planets, just as our ancestors sent settlers from Sirius (our parent planet), and their ancestors sent settlers to Sirius from another star (our grandparent planet).

11. So as the universe continues to increase outward like that, the older sun systems that are much older than Sirius or our earth, that are located closer to the center of the universe, reach perfection first, then their inhabitants help the rest to do the same.

12. Now, the couple that are to become the next Elders - when they are senior citizens at around 7,000 years of age - are informed of their destiny by the ruling King and Queen, and are thus delayed from ascending. They, or anyone else, are never told of their special destiny before then, so that the couple can have a normal life just like all other citizens.

13. They are formally ordained when they are about 25,000 years old. But they don't immediately become Elders at that age. The ordination is so that they can begin their training. Both of them, the man and the woman, are about the same age, the woman usually being younger than the man by only a few years. When they are about 100,000 years old, they will join the Eldership when the ruling Elders ascend.

14. They become the King and Queen of the Tribe of the 2 Elders that just passed away. That Tribe is the 1st and Primary Tribe when its King and Queen are the rulers of the earth, but now, with the passing of the King and Queen, it becomes the last or 12th Tribe with its new King and Queen.

15. It will remain the last Tribe for about 50,000 years. The second Tribe takes over the first position, the 3rd takes over the 2nd and so on.

16. Each couple of Elders choose their own 144 Chiefs. They choose 6 men and 6 women from each Tribe. They don't choose them when they join the Eldership because at that time their Chiefs-to-be are not born yet.

17. The Elders, as I said, live for over 700,000 years. The Chiefs live for about 490,000 years. They choose their Chiefs when they (the Elders) are about 217,000 years old. The Chiefs-to-be that they select at that time are just then senior citizens at 7,000 years old; 72 men and 72 women, soul mate couples.

18. They were getting ready to ascend with the rest of their generation - who are 144,000,000 in number - when the two Elders approach them and inform them that it is not yet time for them to ascend to the ancestor's world.

19. They are informed that they have a mission of many, many more years on earth and will ascend along with their Elders after they have finished ruling the earth, which will be when they (the 144 Chiefs-to-be) are over 490,000 years old. They then accept this honor and become permanently attached to those two Elders as their Sons and Daughters, as they are called, for the rest of their lives.

20. The training of the new 144 Chiefs-to-be starts when they are 7,000 years old. They are trained primarily by their two Elders, but many times also by the reigning Chiefs and all the Chiefs-to-be that are above them, as well as the other Elders.

21. At any given time on earth (under normal circumstances - i.e. not including this age of self-forgetfulness) there are 1,296 Chiefs-in-training, plus the reigning 144 Chiefs, for a total of 1,440 Chiefs. As stated, the Elders choose their Chiefs when they are around 217,000 years old, when their Tribe is in the 10th position.

22. So every couple of Elders from the 10th to the 9th, to the 8th, the 7th and so on to the 2nd Tribe all have Chiefs-to-be. Only the last 2 Tribes - the 11th and 12th Tribe Elders - do not have Chiefs-in-training, but they all have the 12 Chiefs of their Tribe who are part of the 144 ruling Chiefs of the earth.

23. So the youngest Chiefs-in-training are 7,000 years old, being the adopted Sons and Daughters of the 2 Elders of the 10th Tribe, and those of the last 2 Tribes are at least 43,000 years away from being born.

24. Now, every 2 Elders rule for about 50,000 years (sometimes longer, sometimes shorter). The Queen always rules first, for about 25,000 years, followed

by the King for another 25,000 years. I will explain later why the Queen always rules first.

25. So every 50,000 years or so, the 2 rulers will ascend and a new King and Queen will take over, and all the other Elders will advance up, the last (12th) Tribe becoming the 11th, the 11th becoming the 10th and so on up to the 2nd becoming the 1st, and the 1st becoming the last, and remain the last for 50,000 years.

26. At those times of transition, every 50,000 years or so, new Chiefs take over also, as each group of ruling Chiefs ascend to the ancestral world along with their 2 Elders (as well as their Judges, which I will explain later).

27. As every 2 Elders advance up the Eldership, they advance along with their Chiefs-to-be, who, as I said, are permanently attached to them. They continue to teach and train them. Their training is very comprehensive, lasting for over 433,000 years.

28. It is almost as comprehensive as that of the Elders themselves, who remain in training for over 625,000 years before they become the rulers of the earth. As stated, the Elders are ordained when they

are 25,000 years old. That is when their formal training to be Elders begins.

29. After another 75,000 years, they are inducted into the Eldership. Their training continues until they are 650,000 years old, then they become the King and Queen of the earth. They are trained by all the Elders above them, especially the 2 immediately above them. While in this long period of training, they are the King and Queen of their Tribe.

30. Now, when they get to the 10th position, even though they are training their own Chiefs during that time, they nonetheless have 12 Chiefs who are the reigning Chiefs of their Tribe, who were chosen by the reigning King and Queen.

31. As you can imagine, these reigning 12 Chiefs - the ones who belong to the 10th Tribe - are older than the King and Queen of their Tribe (in fact they are older than the Kings and Queens of the last 7 Tribes). Nonetheless, they still function under all the Elders.

32. As I stated, the new Chiefs are selected when they are 7,000 years old. When they get to be 427,000 years old, they select their 144,000 Judges.

They go to the senior citizen generation that is just about to ascend - those that have finished their 7th Great Ritual.

33. From among them they select 144,000 who will become their Judges.   Judges normally live for about 70,000 years.   They are selected when they are 7,000 years old also.   From then on they are trained by their Chiefs as well as by the reigning Judges for a period of 13,000 years, until they are 20,000 years old.

34. At that time the ruling King and Queen ascend. A new King and Queen take over, and so do a new group of 144 Chiefs and their 144,000 Judges.   It is immediately after the ascension of the ruling King and Queen that the new Chiefs-to-be and Judges-to-be are selected, and this happens once every 50,000 years or so.

35. The reason the Elders can only select their Chiefs when they (the Elders) are 217,000 years old, and the Chiefs can only select their Judges when they (the Chiefs) are 427,000 years old, has to do with the lifespan of all three groups of Leaders - the Elders, Chiefs and Judges.

36. In any cycle, all living beings (including animals and plants) are allocated their lifespan. When a planet has reached a state of perfection, it is no longer influenced by cycles, and thus all people and animals no longer die or ascend.

37. At the beginning of the universe there are no cycles yet, as there are no stars, and time does not exist, so the Original People can live as long as they choose. They chose to live for 1 trillion years because that was all the time they needed to create the universe. After that, once the stars have appeared, cycles begin.

38. At that point nature and astrological circumstances dictate the lifespan of all living things, including people, according to the laws set down by the Original People. These laws hold true for a planet until that planet reaches perfection. The laws dictate the lifespan according to the purpose of each cycle.

39. Before this cycle of self-forgetfulness that we are in, the majority of people had a lifespan of 7,000 years in all the cycles. Now and then, as dictated by natural law, a man and woman will be conceived in astrological conditions that dictate a

much longer lifespan - in the case of Chiefs, a lifespan of around 490,000 years.

40. When this happens, the Elders, being the only ones who know this, know that those two will become Chiefs. Like all other living beings, their lifespan is dictated by the astrological circumstances of their conception, and they will live that long because back then there were no accidents or any other kind of premature deaths.

41. Now, it's possible that they (or any other regular person for that matter) can extend their lives beyond their allocated lifespan, but such a thing was so rare that it happened only in situations where it had been planned beforehand by the Elders, as part of their purpose.

42. So the normal way is that when such people incarnate, their lifespan will be according to their astrological conditions. Of course, when I say a lifespan of 490,000 years, this too is an average. In actuality, it could be as low as 480,000 or as high as 500,000 years, but not much more nor less than that.

43. That being the case, and being that the Elders live for about 700,000 years, it stands to reason that

each pair of Elders have to wait until they are about 210,000 years old before their Chiefs-to-be are born; then wait another 7,000 years for them to complete all the 7 Great Rituals of the Black Nation before they can be selected.

44. Once selected, they will be permanently attached to those two Elders and ascend with them when the Elders are about 700,000 years old, and the Chiefs about 490,000 years old.

45. Similarly the Chiefs have to wait till they are about 420,000 years old before their Judges-to-be are born (the Judges have a lifespan of about 70,000 years), and then wait another 7,000 years for them to become senior citizens before they can be ordained.

46. The King and Queen will rule the earth for about 50,000 years from when they are 650,000 years old until they are 700,000 years old. Their Chiefs will reign with them also for 50,000 years from when they are 440,000 years until they are 490,000 years old. So will their Judges also from when they are 20,000 until they are 70,000 years old, and then they will all ascend together.

47. There was a certain ancient tradition that existed among some people in this present 6,000-year cycle. In this tradition, when the king died, all his servants would be killed and buried with him.

48. This custom was a misinterpretation of the true form of this tradition as it was practiced in ancient days. As I said earlier, when the King and Queen ascend, they ascend with their Chiefs and Judges, who are permanently attached to them like their servants.

49. The knowledge of this ancient tradition of the King and Queen ascending with their Chiefs and Judges is what gave rise to the custom among some people of burying a king with all his servants, which is a misinterpretation because the original tradition had to do with conscious ascension, not unconscious death.

50. The Chiefs and Judges took it as a great honor to ascend with their King and Queen, and they willingly laid down their bodies - no one had to kill them.

51. In the present cycle, 6,000 years ago the Judges laid down their bodies to be the bodies of resurrection when they were about 54,000 years

old. They had been Judges for 34,000 years till then. After they resurrect, they will continue to be Judges for another 10,000 years until the rule of the present King comes to an end.

52. When the present King and Queen took over from their predecessors about 40,000 years ago, the Queen ruled first. This is always the case when a new couple takes over - the Queen is the first to rule. The reason is because when our ancient ancestors came here from Sirius, the Queen of that time was the first to rule the planet.

53. Every newly occupied planet is called an infant planet. Such a planet must be nurtured for many thousands of years in order to make it comfortable and ready to accommodate the increasing population.

54. It is sort of like a new house that was just recently built, and the woman of the house has to prepare it and make it ready in the way that only women know how, so it can accommodate the children that will be born. The same is true with new planets.

55. Right at the beginning when the settlers first arrive, the governmental structure operates on a

reduced scale while the population increases. The 144,000 settlers who came from Sirius included 24 Elders, 144 Chiefs, 1,296 Chiefs-to-be, and many other scientists, but no Judges.

56. As the population increases, Judges are selected. When the population reaches the maximum number, then the governmental structure begins to operate full-scale. Even though the Queen was the ruler throughout this whole time of population growth (which can take as long as 7,000 years to reach 1B8M), she actually begins her reign officially when the population reaches 1B8M.

57. So every new planet is always ruled first by a Queen for that reason, then the King follows after. Therefore when the first ruling Queen and King of a new planet hand over to their successors after their 50,000-year reign, it will be the King handing over to the Queen of the next couple.

58. Since that first hand-over 78 trillion years ago, it has always been the same tradition right down to this present Kingdom, when the previous King handed over to our present Queen whose reign ended 15,000 years ago, after she ruled for more than 25,000 years.

59. It was during the reign of that King 50,000 years ago that they decided to prepare the world for the coming era of Yahweh by sending people out to self-isolation and by beginning to de-populate the earth.

60. When that all started, the present group of 144,000 Judges were only about 10,000 years old. They were not yet Judges. Ten thousand years later, their Queen (our present Queen of the earth) took over and ruled for 25,000 years.

61. Then she handed over to her soul mate, our present King, who ruled for 9,000 years before handing the world over to Yahweh. So beginning 50,000 years ago when these Judges were 10,000 years old, they were witnesses to the self-isolation process as well as the de-population process.

62. They lived through the entire degeneration process of our bodies from 12 strands to 2 strands of DNA. Then they saw the rise and fall of Lemuria as well as the rise and fall of Atlantis, right up to 6,000 years ago when they gave up their bodies and made way for Yahweh to take over.

63. They have all that knowledge, experience, and wisdom in their minds; and these minds today are in

self-forgetfulness in the people incarnated as them, who are known as the so-called 144,000 elect.

64. When the 144,000 rise, all that knowledge and history will be resurrected in them when they occupy the bodies of resurrection. They will remember it, as well as the fact that they are full Gods who have already completed all the 7 Great Rituals of the Black Nation.

65. They will join their Chiefs and their King and Queen to rule the earth for another 10,000 years after Yahweh. Then they will all ascend together. We will then get help from our ancestral planet of Sirius to re-balance the coming cycle.

66. This type of help is needed in all situations where a planet, for one reason or another, has to reduce its population. It happens on every planet, for example when it comes time to begin a new cycle of 24 Elders and the continents of the planet have to be re-arranged by natural cataclysms.

67. Then the inhabitants will reduce the population to about 144 million people and go to settle on another nearby planet. When they come back, it is always the case that there are not enough people who have completed all 7 great rituals to fill all the

positions of Chiefs-to-be and Judges-to-be, as well as many other scientific positions that require all 7 Great Rituals.

68. As a result, the ancestral planet (the planet from which their ancestors came, which would be Sirius in our case) will send enough people to fill those positions until the cycle has been re-balanced.

69. So after 10,000 years when our next cycle begins, the King and Queen will ascend with all their Chiefs and Judges. In order to re-balance the cycle, two young Elders, along with 144 Chiefs and 1,296 Chiefs-to-be, and many other scientists, will come from Sirius to help rule our earth and re-establish its balance in the galaxy.

10

THE SEVEN MODES OF
TRANSPORTATION

Yes, as I said before, there are seven modes of transportation that are used by the ancients. The most basic is simply walking. The second is using human-powered vehicles, such as boats.

2. Every country has a system of water canals that run through the towns and larger waterways or rivers that connect different towns. Rowing boats and sailing boats can be seen coursing their way on all the waterways.

3. The third type is animal powered vehicles, such as horse chariots and so on. There are also very large birds that they fly on. These powerful birds

have a wingspan of over 20 feet and can carry two adults or four children a distance of 40 miles without rest at speeds of over 30 miles per hour.

4. These three modes are the most common means of regular transportation among young people, those younger than 1,000 years old who have not yet been initiated into some of the major rituals.

5. These three modes of transportation can be used by all people everyday for personal transportation, as well as to transport various goods that they use in their daily lives. They do not require any particular level of initiation before they can be used.

6. The next four modes are used only by people who have reached a certain level of initiation. The fourth type involves all vehicles that use either electromagnetic or light technology, or a combination of the two.

7. Included among these are the types of vehicles that are earthbound, that look like cars and float a few feet above the ground, and can also go underwater. This category also includes all constructed flying vehicles that are used to fly in

the earth's atmosphere as well as spacecraft that can travel to distant planets.

8. Before any person can use these types of vehicles, they have to be initiated into all the technology. With them, driving a car is not just a matter of practicing and then getting a license. The 'license' must be earned through initiation into all the technology of the vehicle.

9. The person has to have the knowledge to build their own car from scratch, literally. Working in groups, they need to know how to mine the iron ore, how to process it to turn it into a certain type of steel, and how to build a car with it, including the propulsion system and everything else.

10. They have factories that are already equipped for building all types of vehicles. To use the factory, the person has to be initiated into all its technology, and be able to operate the factory equipment from A to Z, starting with the mined ore and ending up with a finished, drivable vehicle. Then and only then does he or she get a 'license' to drive.

11. The same is true for space vehicles, except that in this case they work in groups of 144 or more,

depending on the size of the spacecraft. But each person in the group has to be totally familiar with every aspect of building the spaceship before he or she is given the right to operate it.

12. The fifth type of transportation system is a personal magnetic transportation device that is used only by higher initiates, that I found to be the most amazing of all their transportation devices. It is also used for purposes other than pure transportation.

13. This device is formed at will in just a few seconds by an initiate using the energy that comes out of his or her solar plexus. They are able to harness the earth's magnetic field and form a magnetic sphere of any size using their solar plexus.

14. The most common size seen is about 14 feet tall, and can look like a perfect sphere or an egg shape of any color. It completely surrounds them and they can make the magnetic field envelop every cell of their body. When they do this, it causes the body and everything enveloped by this field to become weightless and become part of the field inside.

15. In other words it neutralizes the magnetic field of every cell in the body until there is no longer any attraction between the body and the magnetic field

of the earth. This neutralizes the earth's magnetic pull on the body, as well as the weight of the atmosphere above the body. These two downward forces are what modern people call 'gravity'.

16. Once the body and everything inside is enveloped like that and is weightless, they then are able to transport themselves by polarizing the magnetic sphere using only their minds, to make it either remain stationary, or be directionally attracted or repelled by the stronger magnetic field of the earth.

17. Using this attraction and repulsion, they are able to move the sphere in any direction within the earth's magnetic field at incredibly high speeds. When they travel long distances across the country or to other countries they fly above the atmosphere and they reach speeds of over 100,000 miles per hour. That means traveling the equivalent of New York to Los Angeles in about 2 minutes.

18. Every cell of their body is totally 'cushioned' within this magnetic sphere, and they can travel silently through the atmosphere at high speed without feeling the effects of the wind. They can use this device on any planet, because all planets have a magnetic field.

19. The most common way for them to use it, is in its invisible state. Thus even when there are dozens of them flying in the same vicinity, as is sometimes the case when large numbers of people arrive at an important gathering, they cannot be seen.

20. But all the residents, even children, are able to perceive them with their higher senses even when they are invisible to the eye. For example when a group of people is expecting someone to arrive in one of these vehicles, you will see them stop and stare at a particular location in the sky, then very soon you will see the sphere 'materialize' as if out of nowhere, then slow down and descend to the ground.

21. It's actually not materializing or dematerializing, they simply change the color to make it invisible when traveling, and then when they are close to landing, they change it back to a visible color.

22. There are other things they can do also with this magnetic sphere. When they make it invisible, you can see through it as if there is nothing there, and not see anything inside it. When a person walks out of it in its invisible state it looks like they just materialized out of a glass pane.

23. Another thing they can do which is even more amazing is they can make it go through objects even with people in it.   You can actually walk right through it and through the people in it.

24. All you will feel as you walk through it is a slight tingle, like static electricity, which stops when you stop moving. In order to take you along, they make the field surround all the cells of your body, and you feel the weightlessness.

25. When they make it invisible and you enter it, you cannot see anything or anyone inside, even your own body.   If it were not for the comfortable 'cushioned' weightless feeling, you could not tell you were in the craft.   You can still see everything outside, but your whole body is totally invisible.

26. I was so fascinated by this effect that at one time I told my Host that I was going to take a mirror with me inside it to find out if I could see a reflection of my face. He just smiled and said yes. Of course this turned out to be foolish on my part as the mirror became invisible along with everything inside the sphere.

27. Using this vehicle, they are able to penetrate into solid mountains, and to the very bottom of the

ocean and even deep down into the earth without having to dig a tunnel. They can enter into the heart of a volcano with it and not feel the slightest rise in temperature. It is by far the most common mode of transportation in and around the earth among those who are initiated into it.

28. They also make smaller ones that they can send remotely anywhere. They use them to see into remote places on earth, under the earth as well as underwater. All these spheres have the ability to magnify anything they come close to, right down to the molecular level.

29. Thus they can penetrate a living body with them and enable themselves to see into the cellular or molecular structure of any living or non-living thing using the smallest of these spheres.

30. The smallest one of these that I saw was about the size of a grain of sand, with a golden color to it. At first I could not see it in the room where a group of us were sitting. Then my Host made it emit a moderately bright light that filled the whole room. Then I was able to locate it at the center of the light.

31. As soon as I focused on it, he turned off the light it was emitting, and then I could clearly see the tiny golden sphere. It moved slowly towards me and I instinctively held up my hand. It floated right up near my finger.

32. My Host said to me to focus on the wall of the room just a few feet in front of me. As I did I saw an enlarged, perfect three dimensional image of my finger in front of the wall, hanging in midair.

33. It was the top part of my finger only, down to the first knuckle. The image grew larger as the tiny sphere moved closer and closer, until it disappeared right inside my finger. Now I could see the insides of my finger - the muscles, sinews and veins surrounding the bone - in perfect living color, about 10 times larger than life-size.

34. The sphere caused a very small pleasant tingling sensation as it moved inside my hand, up my arm and into my torso. At the same time I could see the insides of my body pictured perfectly in front of the wall.

35. My Host then stopped the sphere in front of my heart. I could see the rhythmic movement of my heart beating. The sphere then entered my heart

and stopped near the middle. He then caused the image to enlarge until I could see the individual cells of my heart, with their barely visible rhythmic movements.

36. Finally I felt it move again and it exited through the middle of my chest. The image of my heart remained frozen exactly where it was, enabling me to study it up close, until my host turned it off.

37. All the images were permanently recorded on the sphere. A few days later I was able to mentally project the entire scene again in front of me, and it played the exact same sequence that it recorded before.

38. As I said, these little spheres can also be controlled remotely with mental commands, and be made to project their images while they are many, many miles away. It is my understanding that each sphere can be controlled to move and record only by the person who made it. But the recordings on it can be replayed by anyone who knows the mental commands.

39. As to the volume of images it can record, there seems to be no limit. My Host told me that he had been using the same sphere to study plants, animals

and other things for over 800 years, and said that every recording he made was still on it.

40. The students are divided into groups and each group studies only a particular section of the earth or certain species of plants and animals. Then all the members of the class (the entire generation) share their lessons with one another.

41. There are millions and millions of different species of animals and plants, minerals, metals and crystals etc to be studied. Each student cannot study it all by himself or herself, and that is why they share.

42. The whole generation of 144 million students has to thoroughly know all these things by the time they get to experience the first Great Ritual at around 1,000 years of age. So they have less than 1,000 years to study all of it, and have to divide the studies among the different groups to be able to complete it all.

43. When the first Great Ritual occurs they are able to join their minds and share all their lessons with each other. That way all of them are able to cover every single thing on earth as well as on all the

other planets and celestial bodies in our solar system.

44. One of the purposes of the first Great Ritual is to cause them to know every single thing that exists in our solar system, and they cannot know it until they finish studying all of it with their electromagnetic light spheres.

45. The spheres provide them not only with images, but they also transmit all the properties of the thing they record. That includes all five physical properties of sensation (image, sound, smell, taste and texture) as well as super-physical properties.

46. Now, when the sphere records and transmits a property such as texture in a three-dimensional image, it is transmitted directly as electromagnetic properties, meaning the actual unique vibrational frequencies of the object. As you already know, every sensation has a unique vibration, or what we may call a unique electro-magnetic signature.

47. So the image that is transmitted that you then see in front of you, is only an electro-magnetic light representation of the object; even though it is so perfect that it looks real, it does not have any solidity, and you can move your hand through it.

But when you touch it, you will feel its texture. So you can feel the texture of a person's heart, or whatever the object may be.

48. When your hand touches the image, the recorded sense properties interact with the electromagnetic properties of your skin, causing you to feel the object's texture. In a similar way they record smells, sounds, and even taste. When you put your nose on the image, you will smell the smell of your own heart.

49. Thus not only are you able to see every detail of your heart, but you can feel the texture of every part of it, smell it, hear its muted sounds, and even taste it.

50. Since the only thing transmitted in the image is an electromagnetic signature and not the actual chemicals that make up the object, that means you can safely touch, smell or taste the recorded image of any object, even those that are inedible and would otherwise make you sick.

51. In the setting I was in, with only a small group of people, I was able to walk to the image to touch it. In normal circumstances when they present their

studies to large groups of people, they do not approach the object like I did.

52. They use a certain type of crystal that they attach to their upper arm, around their bicep, using a bicep bracelet make of silver or gold.

53. The crystal receives transmissions directly from the image and passes them to the person's electromagnetic biosphere, or what is called the aura. So all the people in the arena watching the presentation are able to touch or smell the image - as well as get its super-physical properties at will simply by giving a mental command to their arm crystal.

54. The people make their remote-controlled electromagnetic light spheres when they are about 80 to 90 years old, soon after finishing the ritual for the creation of life. Each person makes his or her tiny sphere only once, and keeps it for about a thousand years. They do not deteriorate, being made of magnetism, electricity and light.

55. They store it in a small indentation on another crystal that they attach to their upper or lower arm bracelet, or sometimes on a finger ring. Women

usually attach it to a necklace, a head bracelet or a wrist bracelet.

56. Then during the next 900 years or so, until they reach 1,000 years of age, they use it as the main tool for all their biochemical studies, as well as the study of minerals, metals and crystals on earth and all over the solar system.

57. They complete all of this physical study by the time they reach 1,000 years of age. Then they are ready to take part in the first Great Ritual. This Ritual will help them to consolidate all of that knowledge and make it a part of their being.

58. After they complete it, they no longer have a need to use the small spheres. They are able from then on to use other, more advanced methods of study, which enable them to expand their studies beyond our solar system, to encompass all the star systems in our galaxy.

59. For young people, those under 1,000 years of age, the spheres are a popular way to communicate with others. They do have telepathic abilities starting at a very young age, but they are limited only to the exchange of thought conversations,

without the ability to transmit sensations or images of their surroundings.

60. So they use the spheres, which act somewhat like video telephones, except that they are three dimensional and do not need a screen, and can also transmit sensations.

61. When a person communicates with another, they will see his image and as much of the surroundings as the other person lets into the image, and also get all the sounds, smells etc using their arm crystal.

62. But all these sensations are only recorded properties. In other words, when you touch the image of a person and feel their skin, you are only touching a recorded sensation. The person does not feel you touching them.

63. They conference with one another in large groups in arenas that are specifically built for this purpose. There they set up communications with multiple groups all over the world.

64. They share their studies on a monthly basis or more often if something important is discovered by one of the groups and needs to be shared immediately.

65. The sixth mode of transportation is de-materialization, which is used by the higher initiates to travel to other places in the universe by de-materializing their bodies and re-materializing at their chosen destination.

66. Then finally their highest form of transportation is mental travel, where they leave their bodies behind and go to other regions of the universe and use the bodies of their twin souls, or even go to other universes where they are able to instantly make new bodies for themselves.

67. **Brother B, you told me when you go to the past, you can only observe but cannot change or influence the events because the past has already happened. So how can the Host allow you to take a mirror into the craft? Is that not changing the events of the past.**

68. No, brother _ . Not at all. Remember I already told you that the First Self knows all the details of your life, including your (His) entire future, to the very end of the universe. He knows every single detail of all that will happen to you, and how you will react. That is part of the learning experience.

69. There is an ideal path of experience that you can follow to gain knowledge and experience in any given lifetime. But no person ever follows the ideal path, simply because each one is a unique personality. So you 'color' or modify that ideal path with your unique personality.

70. But no matter how much you deviate from the ideal straight path, the First Self is always there to guide you back on to the path, gently and lovingly, as you well know.

71. At the same time, the First Self also knows, given your personality, just how much you will deviate from the 'straight and narrow', so to speak. He knows your personality - your soul - better than you know it yourself.

72. Now that means my First Self knew that I would do such a foolish thing as to take a mirror with me. He knew this thousands of years ago, before the personality that I am was even conceived. It is literally true that God knows the end from the beginning, and every point in-between.

73. So thousands of years ago, when my First Self was incarnated as that Host, one day he simply smiled and took a mirror into the magnetic vehicle

to 'find out' if he could see his face. The Host at that time was most likely not totally aware why he would do something that foolish, but felt a calling from his First Self to do it, you see.

74. And so he just smiled and did it. His friends probably knew this was something being orchestrated by his First Self. They know from experience when someone does something out of the ordinary that the First Self is inspiring the person to do it.

75. So thousands of years later, meaning now when the First Self is incarnated as me, and sent me to the past, I behaved exactly as my personality dictated I would, which was to take a mirror inside the craft.

76. When the Host heard this thought he just smiled and in his mind came the answer, 'go ahead', directed to 'me' thousands of years later. The communication was really between my mind and the mind of the First Self and is not affected by time or space, but the actions themselves are fixed in the past and do not change.

77. Mind communication goes on all the time between the person and his/her First Self. Some of

it is you asking questions and the First Self answering, and some of it is your future selves that you will be hosting thousands, even millions of years after you have ascended, coming to the past and asking those questions, and receiving answers from the same First Self.

78. Have you ever found yourself explaining things to yourself in your mind, things that you already know very well? When that happens usually it's because you are being inspired by your First Self to do so.

79. Long after you have ascended, your spiritual descendent will possibly come through Ditoro into your mind and be hosted by you. He will ask questions, and those things you are explaining to yourself today, will be the answers he gets at that time.

80. Can you now see how the entire event was orchestrated by one who knows the future in every detail? He caused the Host to behave in a way that would allow me, using his body, to take a mirror into the vehicle, knowing this was exactly what I would wish to do thousands of years before I was even conceived. Is this clear?

81. Yes i think i get it. I'm gonna sleep on it, but I think I get the gist of it. Also you say 'my face'. Do you mean the face of the Host?

82. It's my face. I am one with the Host. His thoughts are my thoughts, I know him as myself and myself as him, there is no separation whatsoever. When I 'tell him' something, I am simply thinking a thought to myself, and when the answer comes, I know it comes from the First Self, who is responsible for uniting the two of us as one.

11

BIOLOGICAL

FUNCTIONS

b lkroots, did the ancients go to the bathroom?

2. You may find this hard to believe, but the reason you go to the bathroom is really to remind you that you are not eating right. You are eating the wrong food; food that creates gas and residue in your stomach and bladder; you are eating too much of it, and you are eating too often on an improper schedule.

3.   So it's really a safety mechanism made by the body to remind you of all those things. It's exactly like when you see ants in your home. That means you have food where it's not supposed to be, and it could create a health hazard and harm you and your family.

4.   So the ants, roaches, rats etc come in not only to get that food, but to act as a warning to you that you are putting your health at risk, and you need to clean up your house.

5.   The same is true with gas and constipation. It's the body's way of telling you that you need to clean up your act and start eating right. When you do that, then you will no longer need to be warned in that way. Your stomach will settle down.

6.   Your body will become healthier, and you will approach a state of health that is closer to what we had in our ancient perfect bodies. Of course you will not achieve that 100% because our present bodies have some inherent weaknesses that we inherited from mixing with the weaker races.

7.   These have to do with the fact that our 12 strands of DNA cannot be as fully active in these bodies as they were in our ancient bodies. But it's

possible to activate our DNA to the point where we can live a healthy life for 1,000 years.

8. The more perfect your health becomes in this body, the closer you will be to being able to resurrect consciously in one of the perfect bodies. The closer you get to that state, the less you will need safety mechanisms to warn you about the effects of unhealthy practices and unhealthy eating habits.

9. Ultimately, these safety mechanisms are designed to prod you in a particular direction, given that we are in a state of self-forgetfulness. So the body has created all these discomforts to constantly urge us to keep working on our body and mind to overcome the self-forgetful state.

10. That is the ultimate purpose of all these mechanisms, including the fact that we need to go to the bathroom. When we reach that state where we are no longer self-forgetful, when we know who we are and are able to consciously communicate with our Higher Self, then all the things in our body that serve only the purpose of being a safety mechanism will no longer be needed.

11. Being in constant contact with the First Self is all we need to live in harmony with everything around us; we will no longer need roaches, rats, stomach constipation, etc to remind us to move in the right direction.

12. So it should be clear then as to why the ancients did not experience any of these things. They were not in self-forgetfulness, hence they did not need external stimuli to prod them. This is true not only of external stimuli; it is true also of how their bodies were constructed internally.

13. Their bodies did not have the types of things we have in our bodies, whose only function is to warn us of the dangers of bad habits; and the reason being simply because they did not engage in bad habits. When I say "the types of things" I mean specific things like the bladder and the lower intestine which leads to the anal opening.

14. The only purpose of the anal opening is to let out the residues left behind when we eat more than we need to, or eat the wrong food as well as eating on a wrong schedule. If we ate the right food at the right time and only as much as we needed, there would not be any residue left in the stomach and bladder.

15. People assume that urinating and defecating are an absolute biological necessity just because they see that all people and animals engage in this biological act. This is simply not true.

16. These activities are the direct result of having residue in the body, and nothing else. They are not a biological necessity. We make residue when we end up with more food in the body than we need.

17. This is true for both people and animals. Animals don't have a choice in the matter; they just follow what people do. When people started to overeat 50,000 years ago, and to eat the wrong foods, animals then started to do the same.

18. Had we not done this, there would be no residue left in our bodies after we eat, hence there would be no need for a bladder or an anal opening. All the food we eat would be converted directly to energy.

19. This happens with plants today. When they take in minerals and water, all of it is turned into energy for the growth of the plant. There is no residue. That means they naturally take in only what they need.

20. This was the case as well with the ancients. They ate and drank only as much as they needed and all of it was turned into energy, leaving no residue. So they did not urinate or defecate. Their bodies did not have an anal opening.

21. Of course, someone may say, if they ate food and none of it came out as residue back to the earth, then would that not deplete the earth? Eating all that food and never giving any of it back to mother earth it would seem like we would eventually eat up the whole earth. After all, food is matter, and all matter must be recycled and re-circulated.

22. That is actually a good question. The answer is that energy is also part of the recycling process. In the universe, matter is converted to energy all the time, and then back to matter again. We have an energy body, also called our body of action.

23. So the food they ate was converted into energy in the action body, and when the energy is used for material activities, then that energy is recycled back again into matter such that the overall balance is maintained.

24. All the food and liquid they took into the body got into their bloodstream to energize the body. Some of the liquid of course is used to lubricate the eyes and mouth and so on, and some came out as sweat to cool down the body when they had to exert too much.

25. Sweat is not an elimination of residue, but a necessary cooling mechanism. Even so, they did not sweat copiously like people do today. They would only get tiny sweat beads on their extremely fine skin whose pores are so small that on first look you would think their skin had no pores at all.

26. Moreover, it was simply not possible for them to eat more than they needed. If they were to try - which of course they never did - then the body would reject the food and it would come back out of their mouths. I'm sure you have seen a baby rejecting food like that.

27. So they never did that after they passed their infancy. They learnt when they were infants that the body cannot be force-fed when it has had enough. Because of this, they were incapable of having residue in their bodies, and that is the reason why they did not have an anal opening.

28. The anal opening and the bladder began to develop 50,000 years ago when people deliberately lost their proper eating habits. Over a period of many thousands of years they slowly but surely forced small extra amounts of food and liquid into their stomachs and forced themselves to hold it down.

29. The body responded by slowly developing a pouch to store the extra food and another for the extra liquid. That is how the lower intestine and the bladder were formed. As time went on, the pressure of the residue in this lower intestine forced an opening to form so that the excess food could be expelled.

30. With the bladder, there was already an opening so the body just formed an extra valve to regulate the two channels, one for semen and the other for urine in males.

31. Then animals got their instructions from the magnetic mind of the planet to do the same. It all started slowly and was fully developed after a period of about 20,000 years.

32. This opening serves no other purpose than to remind us that we are in a less than perfect state

and we need to continue working to perfect ourselves. When we do, then it will no longer be needed and will cease to exist.

33. This long description that I made here about the purpose of this biological function is really to try and illustrate something parallel but more important, which is that the existence of the light races serves exactly the same purpose.

34. They are here to remind us of our state of self-forgetfulness. Everything that comes out of their mouths is exactly like that residue, and should be treated as such. Once we remember who we are, they too will no longer be needed.

35. When God has completed the creation of the universe and the universe has reached absolute perfection, he will unite with that perfection and take it back into himself. He does not unite with what is less than perfect, or that which is still seeking absolute perfection.

36. When the universe reaches perfection, all the plants and animals and objects that will be in it at that time will have reached a state of absolute perfection, where they no longer evolve or die. What cannot be perfect will not be in the physical

universe. It will long be extinct, and that includes the light races and all their progeny.

12

SECONDARY
UNIVERSES

Brother Blackroots, I have a couple of questions... what happened to the past universe we came from? after it fills its mandate and comes to an end, does it just disintergrate?

2. I'm really fascinated by the idea you put forth of a universe existing 'within' the first earth. Does this mean only the first earth is a universe? When thinking on this, I have come

to the conclusion that each and every planet is a universe, similarly, hence the whole concept of 'infinity' within 'infinity'. Am i off track? Please elaborate. Thank you in advance.

3. You are right on track my brother, and to tell you the truth I am quite impressed that you were able to figure that out independently. Keep it up brother, and you will continue to get answers from your intuition about things that are more amazing than any person who is a product of this modern age can ever imagine.

4. The past universe does not disintegrate. Once it reaches perfection, it remains in that state of perfection forever. All its energies have reached a state of perfect balance and harmony. All the planets have their axes reach a vertical position; they no longer wobble on their axes to make seasons, so they are all in an eternal spring like the first earth.

5. All the living creatures and plants in it no longer evolve or die. They have reached the top of their evolutionary ladder and continue to exist forever in a state of perfection.

6. So these universes are still there, but they are not permanently occupied by people. They are occupied only by non-human creatures that the Gods created to live in them. New people only go there to study them and gain knowledge about the past.

7. When our universe reaches its mandate and comes to an end, we will all enter into the state of divine unity where each one of us as individuals knows himself/herself as the one and only God.

8. We will comprehend all the universes of the past since the beginning that has no beginning. We, the new personalities who have never existed before, will encompass them all in that timeless moment and absorb all that they are into ourselves and use it as wisdom when we create the next universe.

9. So you see, each new universe encompasses and includes all the wisdom gained from all past universes in their infinitude.

10. As to your second question about infinity within infinity, it's like this: the universe we live in at present can be called a primary universe, for lack of a better word.

11. A primary universe is one that is created immediately after another primary universe has fulfilled its purpose and has come to an end, and has become the first earth of the new universe.

12. That old universe is called a past universe, or the universe that existed immediately before our universe. It too was a primary universe.

13. There are other universes that are not primary, but may be called secondary universes. A secondary universe is a universe that is created from the atoms of the planets of the primary universe. These atoms are located on what may be called the 2nd level, 3rd level, 4th level (of 'atomic' structure) and so on back to infinity.

14. Secondary universes are created within the solar system planets that were formed around the first earth by the condensation of God's mind. As a matter of fact, that is part of the reason why God condenses new solar systems out of his/her mind, precisely so that there will be trillions upon trillions of new planets that will become secondary universes on these multiple levels below.

15. So how are these secondary universes created? First of all, they are created by the people that

inhabit the new solar systems of the primary universe, such as our ancestors when they came here from Sirius.

16. The inhabitants of the first earth do create secondary universes also, they create them within other planets that are part of their solar system.

17. Soon after the settlers occupy a new solar system, after about 7 thousand years when they have settled down on their new earth and made it a comfortable home, a group of 144,000 will get together and formulate a plan for the creation of a secondary universe out of the atoms of their own planet and other planets in their solar system.

18. These secondary universes are created on the 3rd level of the earth's atomic structure (and below the 3rd level as well). They go to the second level (the level just below us), and choose a suitable planet. Then descend into the 2nd level of that planet, which would be the 3rd level from the point of view of our earth.

19. The secondary universes are created only by senior citizens who have completed all 7 great rituals of the Black Nation and have become full Gods. They engage in this creation as their last

project before they ascend. They form a group of 144,000 people to take part in this creative endeavor. As I noted earlier, these universes are not primary universes; they have a different purpose than that of a primary universe, and thus do not require the participation of all 1b8m Gods.

20. Since the planets of those 3rd level universes are themselves made of atoms, and those atoms as well are made of atoms, there is no end to the number of levels within a single planet.

21. The creators are able to descend further and further into the 'atomic' structure of the planet and find more universes within, such that every generation of senior citizens is able to locate a level where they can engage in these creations.

22. The first inhabitants of our earth, the 144,000 that came from Sirius, created the very first secondary universe to ever be created within our earth; they created it on the 3rd level of 'atomic' structure of our planet.

23. Then after our earth's population had increased, another group of 144,000 descended also and they created another secondary universe, and then later a third group did the same, and so on and so on.

24. It has been going on now for 78 trillion years, and our ancestors have reached many levels below our earth's atomic structure. The levels that exist within the earth's atomic structure are beyond the numbers of modern mathematics.

25. The movement of the planets within the earth's atoms are of the order of 7,000 trillion years per second. In other words, when one second has passed on earth, over 7,000 trillion years have passed on the 2nd level, the level just below us.

26. On the level below that, i.e. two levels below us, the planets orbit around their sun in the order of 7,000 tr x 7,000 tr years per second, or 49 million trillion trillion years in one second of earth time. Of course, this does not mean the planets hurtle around their sun at unimaginable speeds.

27. They revolve around their sun just like our earth revolves around our sun, so when you are on that level, the planetary movement appears just like normal. But if you could see them from earth you would see them going around 49 mil tr tr times in one second.

28. That incredibly large time differential is precisely the reason why the Gods create secondary

universes on the 3rd level (and below), and not on the 2nd. Remember, each universe takes about 875 trillion trillion trillion years to reach completion, and for the 3rd level that is only about 6 to 7 months on earth.

29. On the 2nd level the time would be way too long, way beyond the 7,000-year lifespan of the creators. (What is to us the 2nd level, will become the 3rd level for the people of the next universe, and they will create there).

30. Thus they are able to create a brand new universe on the 3rd level and see it reach completion in its allotted time of 875 trillion trillion trillion years, which is how long it takes for it to reach perfect harmony of all its universal energies. And during all those trillions of years, only 7 months pass here on earth.

31. When they decide to create a secondary universe, they cooperate in a group of 144,000 as I said; 72,000 men and 72,000 women, or 72,000 soul mate couples. The first time they descend to the 3rd level, they all 'sleep' for 3 days in a temple they call the Temple of universe creation.

32. This temple has 144,000 stone 'coffins', or what modern Egyptologists call a sarcophagus in which they lay down their bodies.   The temple priests attending to their bodies are able to use the magnetic quality of the stone 'coffins' to preserve those bodies in perfect comfort during the 3-day 'rest' period. The bodies lay in there without touching the stone, floating in a soft magnetic field.

33. So they do not descend to the 3rd level in their physical bodies, but only in their minds, sort of like a group lucid dream.   They lie down in these 'coffins', and use the properties of the stone to facilitate the unity of their minds and the coherence of their 'lucid dream', for lack of a better word, and then all descend mentally as one.

34. That first time, they will live continuously on the 3rd level for a trillion years, exactly as our ancestors, the original Gods, did when they created this universe. But when that entire trillion years has passed on the 3rd level, only a fraction of a micro-second has passed on earth.

35. Nonetheless, they have to 'sleep' for the entire 3 days in order for their bodies, especially their brains, to acclimate to their minds upon their 'return', because the mind comes back with a trillion

years' worth of new information, experiences and wisdom, and all that has to be harmonized in their bodies.

36. If they wake up too soon and it's not properly harmonized, there is the possibility that some of that knowledge would be lost in the brain's memory circuits. This harmonization is done using special rituals that are performed by the temple priests who attend to their bodies while they are 'gone', so to speak (the English language here is beginning to lack quite a bit, making it difficult to convey these concepts).

37. When they get there, they live in new bodies that they create instantly upon arrival on the central planet of that universe, which they use as their first earth, or headquarters. Then they organize the sun systems of that universe until they attain a set-up that is in accordance with their plan.

38. Unlike with the creation of a primary universe, they do not create new sun systems by condensation of the mind. All the sun systems of that universe already exist. So they rearrange them according to plan, and this takes approximately a trillion years, during which they live continuously.

39. They also create perfect plants and animals on that central earth, exactly as is done during the creation of a primary universe. Then at the end of the trillion years, they create new beings to populate their universe, then they 'return' to earth.

40. The beings that they create in these secondary universes are not what would be called human. They are not animals either, but are somewhat midway between human and animal. They are much more intelligent than the highest animals. In fact they are created right from the beginning having maximum intelligence.

41. That means they are able to take custodianship of their universe from their makers and run that universe with 100% efficiency, as if they are an integral part of nature. That is actually what they are; they are elements of nature in semi-human form, with the full capacity of nature's intelligence.

42. These universes are created fundamentally for the purpose of being 'the gardens of the ancestors', where they cultivate their original ideas and bring them into physical manifestation. They are also created for the purpose of being studied by future generations.

43. These perfect intelligent creatures in these universes are created primarily for the purpose of transforming those universes to please their creators. The transformations they come up with are totally original, coming from their own native intelligence, but are 'colored' by the intentions of their creators, so to speak.

44. Thus when they make these improvements, not only are such modifications pleasing to all who visit, but are at the same time a pleasant surprise even to their very creators.

45. These creatures do not have a creative component within them, i.e. they are not able to come up with new creations. They can only improve what has been given to them, and the improvements they can make are without limit. Also, they are not able to reproduce themselves.

46. Their numbers can only be increased by their creators, and this does happen when the creators decide that more of the beings are needed. Once they are created, they never die. They live forever, being sustained by certain pure energies of their universe.

47. At the end of the trillion years when the creators have finished with their universal set-up, the universe at that point will continue 'automatically', following the natural laws established by the creators. After the creators leave, the creatures then take over as permanent custodians of the universe and proceed to modify and improve it in line with the natural laws.

48. These creatures also have a very powerful mental ability to preserve the different stages that the universe goes through as it changes. In other words, they are able to preserve a 'copy' of the universe exactly as it was in the beginning, and at every stage after that when modifications were made.

49. They use their mental powers to turn these preserved stages into what may be called 'museums', for lack of a better word. When visitors arrive in their universe, they are able to present these 'museum' stages to them in sequence, showing where they started and all the modifications they have made.

50. Not only that, but by this same power, they are able to project into the future for many billions of years to reveal what their next improvements will

look like. So even those people who visit such a universe closer to its beginning point are able to see what it will look like at different stages in the future.

51. These 'museum' stages are not just a projection though. They actually are able to recreate any part of their universe as it was back in time. Thus people who visit there will spend long periods in a past stage of the universe that they like, or go through all the stages from the beginning, observing all the major changes that have taken place, right down to the present, as well as project into the future to see upcoming changes.

52. As I said, only senior citizens who have completed all 7 great rituals are able to create these secondary universes. But all other people are able to visit these universes as 'tourists', so to speak.

53. As soon as the creators 'return' from the 3rd level, there is a rush by all the younger citizens to descend and see what has been newly created. Top priority is given to the youngest, those who will be descending for the first time, because it is much easier for them to descend to the 2nd and 3rd level

than it is to descend to levels that are below the 3rd.

54. They have to complete at least one of the 7 Great Rituals before they can have the ability to descend below the 3rd level. Even going to the 3rd level, they are accompanied by some senior citizens.

55. When they descend, they use the same Temple of creation, and go in groups of 144,000, plus the Teachers who accompany them.

56. They 'sleep' in the temple for 3 days, and when they get to the secondary universe, they spend as much time as they need to tour the entire creation, and gain as much knowledge as they need about how universes are created; knowledge that they will put to use when they become senior citizens and create their own secondary universe.

57. They can be there for as short as 7,000 years, or much, much longer than that; yet they will 'awaken' on earth after 3 days regardless of how short or how long they were in the secondary universe.

58. During this 3-day period when they are down there, they will usually split into smaller groups,

some people will spend a long time in one or two universes, while others will spend short periods in many different universes, spreading across to many planets of the 2nd level that have been turned into secondary universes.

59. Those who are able to, who have completed some of the Great Rituals, will descend even further down into universes that were created trillions of years ago by our remote ancestors.

60. When our primary universe comes to an end, all the knowledge and wisdom gained from all the endless secondary universes will become part of the plan for creating the next universe, just as our universe was created by incorporating the wisdom gained from all the secondary and primary universes of the past.

13

MORE ON THE BIG BANG

Modern scientists claim that the universe is expanding from the big bang. They look through their telescopes and use other modern methods to deduce that the galaxies are moving away from the earth and from each other.

2. From these deductions they come to the conclusion that the universe must be expanding as a result of their big bang, which says that the universe started as an explosion and all celestial bodies continue to move outward in all directions because of that explosion.

3. This is an erroneous interpretation of scientific data. Their perception is correct that the galaxies are moving away from the earth and from each other, but to use that information to jump to the conclusion that the universe must be expanding, is an error.

4. I will try to explain the situation by using an example that is close to home and is therefore much easier to comprehend.

5. Let us say hypothetically there are short-lived beings on Mars who only live for three months. Their scientists look through their telescopes at our earth, Venus, Jupiter, and other planets.

6. Let us say the first time they look, the earth happens to be moving away from Mars, as it actually does periodically. And let us assume also that at the same period, Venus and Jupiter are also moving away from Mars, as they also do periodically.

7. Now because these scientists are very short-lived, having a lifespan of only three months, during their observations they will see the earth moving away from Mars for the entire duration of their lifespan, because the earth will move around the sun away from them for about three months, then

turn and move in another direction for another three months, and so on until it completes a full revolution in one year.

8. But because these scientist only live for 3 months, they will not be able to see the earth coming around and moving back closer to Mars. They can only see it moving away in their lifetime.

9. And so if they are like modern earth scientists they will come to the conclusion that our solar system is expanding because the planets are moving away from each other.

10. To see the situation as it really is, using only their telescopes, they would have to wait many lifetimes until other scientists collect more data, and see the earth coming around and back toward Mars, and then move away again, then come back again etc, as it revolves round and round the sun.

11. Then they would come to the correct conclusion that the solar system is not expanding, but rather the planets move around the sun, sometimes going away from Mars, and other times approaching Mars.

12. That is precisely the situation with all the galaxies. The only problem is that the revolutionary

circuits of galaxies are so large that it would take millions of years for earth scientists to collect all the necessary data using their modern methods.

13. At the present time, no matter how long they make their observations, they will only see the galaxies that they are watching, moving away. They will not see them make a turn and come around and start moving towards our galaxy.

14. They will seem to continue to be moving away forever in the same direction because their orbital circuit around the galactic sun takes millions of years to complete.

15. The modern methods of astronomical observation are extremely inadequate for observing celestial bodies whose periods of revolution are millions or billions of years long. This in itself would not necessarily lead to all these erroneous conclusions.

16. Using proper logic, they could still discover the truth, but the problem is they are handicapped by previous pre-conceived notions, namely their theory of the big bang.

17. As soon as they observed that some galaxies were moving away from our galaxy, they immediately took that as confirmation of their big bang theory. According to this theory, the universe must indeed expand because it started as a localized explosion, and the nature of an explosion is to expand outward in all directions.

18. Because of this false theory, they are logically handicapped. It prevents them from using logic to see that galaxies behave exactly like planets in a solar system.

19. They revolve back and forth around their galactic suns, those in one galactic group moving away from those in another group for millions of years, then moving towards each other for millions more.

14

More On Consciousness

A ll things exist as vibration in the Mind of God. We say that consciousness itself, or the mind, is vibration. The Consciousness of God is One Vibration and from this comes the infinitude of vibrations, or frequencies, that make up all of existence.

2. This includes space. It too is vibrations, or distinct frequencies within the mind. Therefore, space does not exist separately somewhere; it exists only in the mind, as do all things. They only go 'out

there' in space when we project them and perceive them.

3. This leads of course to the obvious question: If all things exist only in the mind as vibrations, or what we call thoughts, then where are they when the mind is not thinking of them, or not projecting them?

4. The answer is just as obvious, although it may be hard to accept. The fact of the matter is that things exist only when we perceive them. When we don't perceive them, they simply cease to exist in space. If I happen to be in my town interacting with people and perceiving the usual things that exist in that space, that is all that exists for me.

5. Everything else, the entire universe that is not within my perception, ceases to exist. When I travel to the next town and perceive different things and different people, then my town and all the people and things I left behind cease to exist. At that moment, my entire universe is made up of only that which is within my perception.

6. Now, the beauty of it is that even though my town has ceased to exist, its 'timeline', so to speak, continues in my mind, as do the timelines of all

other things, i.e. everything that is not currently in my perception.

7. By that I mean things will continue to age accordingly, as if they still exist in space. So when I return to my town, say 10 years later, it will come back to existence as soon as it comes back into my perception, and it will be in its proper time slot.

8. The people will have aged by 10 years. Some buildings will be gone, replaced by new ones maybe. Trees and other plants will be gone or be different, some people will have died and others will have been born etc.

9. So as soon as I bring it back into existence by perceiving it, it will automatically fall into the proper time slot which is naturally and effortlessly calculated by my mind.

10. And that is because even though it had ceased to exist in space, it continued to exist in my mind. My mind is then able to age everything properly, and make the changes that I now see, because the Mind, being One, knows the beginning, middle, and end of all things.

11. It is able to allocate to all things their proper time slots and places in space even when I, the person, does not perceive those things.

12. This allocation results in a sense of continuity. It is this sense of continuity that gives the impression that things continued to exist even when I did not perceive them.

13. But such is not the case; they simply do not exist when I don't perceive them. The entirety of existence consists only of that which is within my perception at any given moment. Nothing else exists outside of that.

14. Someone of course could say, well, when you left the town, other people remained there, not to mention all the animals etc that are also able to perceive, and since they continued to perceive the town, then it continued to exist in space, just like it did when you perceived it.

15. The hard truth is that it really does not matter what anyone else perceives. As long as it is not within your perception, it does not exist. If you do not see those people perceiving the town, how do you know that they are perceiving it?

16. You do not know this for a fact, you only surmise that they must be there and must be perceiving, but you do not see that as an actuality. Think of it like this.

17. Let's suppose that the day after you leave that town, God wipes it off the map entirely, and no one ever tells you that; then a day before you come back, God puts it back in its place (and in the proper time, with everything aged accordingly, and the people's memories adjusted accordingly).

18. If you have the belief that things exist outside of your perception, you will incorrectly conclude that the town existed all the time in that space, even though it actually ceased to exist.

19. That is precisely what happens with everything that leaves your perception. God does not have to use any energy to wipe it off the face of the universe. It naturally and effortlessly ceases to exist in space as soon as you cease to perceive it.

20. Later when you get back and talk to your friends and they tell you how things 'were' while you were gone, you are actually creating that history anew as you hear it. All those people telling you what went on in your absence, are being projected by you and

being perceived by you in the present, and that past is being created anew.

21. If the past they are telling you about is true, it is being taken directly from the One Mind by you and being projected out so you can perceive it and experience it now. You are making it exist in space right there.

22. The above-mentioned will help to explain why it is possible to mentally go back in time and experience the 'past'. When we travel back in time, we create the past using our own mind. It does not exist in space anywhere before then.

23. To bring it to existence, we take the images of the 'past' from the One Mind and project them out so we can perceive them and experience them. So it is not as if the past really exists at some point in 'time' or some place in space. It does not.

24. It will exist in space and time only when you project it outward and perceive it. And if you perceive it truly, then it will be the true 'past', exactly as it exists in the One Mind of God. God has already set it in place by giving us the experiences of the present, the now, in the manner that we experience the now.

25. This now that we experience is related to the 'past', which we must also experience. And that is why the 'past' is fixed and unchangeable, because it is the 'mother', so to speak, of the present.

26. It has to be exactly as it is recorded in God's mind in order for it to give rise to the present we are now experiencing. So all people who travel to the true past, will see exactly the same past.

27. So this 'past' exists only when we project it and perceive it, just like the present. Therefore it can only be perceived in the now, in the present moment. In fact, NOW is the only time that exists because what I am perceiving now is all that exists.

28. Depending on the stage of one's development (or initiation), there are different methods available of how to get to the past. The simplest for initiates is to go through a Gatekeeper and use that mind to see the past exactly as the Gatekeeper sees it.

29. Some initiates that are more advanced may not need the help of a Gatekeeper as they can create a means for themselves to independently perceive any time in the past.

30. So when I get to that point in the past I actually re-create it exactly as it was then, but because I perceive it NOW, it actually exists now, in the present, at the time that I perceive it. The Gatekeeper who assists me, is my projection as well, just like everything else I perceive.

31. So the past must be created anew in order to be perceived. As you can imagine, this requires a complete stillness of the mind in order to be able to receive the true images of the past from the Higher mind.

32. If one's mind is not totally still, there is the possibility of inserting one's own imaginations and adding scenes to the past that did not happen. But with enough training, the process becomes very simple and effortless, and one is then able to make the past exist again in the present.

33. But, to repeat, this 'past' does not exist until I project it and perceive it. Again, I could hear someone say, what about other initiates who have traveled to the past before you, and even taught you how to do the same, are you saying their experiences are not real, since the past will exist only when you perceive it?

34. And again I will say, the 'perceptions' and 'experiences' of other people do not matter to you as long as they are separate from you. The only perceptions that make up reality are your own.

35. When other people tell me that they went to the past, that is not my experience therefore as long as I am a separate person I have no way of knowing it as actual fact.

36. Them standing before me and the stories that they tell me and the valuable teachings that they impart to me, and all the initiations that they so lovingly put me through, all these things are actually me projecting them into existence exactly the same way I project and perceive everything else.

37. Similarly the only way for the past to exist and become part of my experience is for me to receive it from the Mind in a true form and project it. Then and only then does it come into existence, and then I can perceive and experience it.

38. The ancient Pyramids, the amazing monuments that we see, the incredible ancestors that we hear about today, all these things are the daughters of a mother who does not yet exist for me.

39. But I have a definite idea of what that mother looks like because I have the daughter to look at. This daughter guides us to the correct images when it is time for us to travel to the past.

40. We do so in the right way and see the past exactly as it 'was', in other words, we create it in time and space exactly as it should be, because we are able to receive the proper images of the 'mother' (the past), having experienced the daughter (having experienced the present).

41. So you see, nothing else exists in space except what is here and now in your perception. Not the past, not even things of the present that are outside your perception.

42. All the talk about how large the universe is, how much 'matter' is in it, how much energy, how long it has been around, etc, all these things do not yet exist for you if you do not perceive them. They will exist only when you perceive them.

43. So at this moment as you are where you are, there are no billions of galaxies in existence hanging in space 'out there' somewhere where you cannot see them. All these things are still in the Mind as thoughts, waiting for you to perceive them. When

you do, then and only then do they come into existence.

44. All the great ancestors you have heard about who lived in the past, do not exist yet for you. They are waiting in the One Mind for you to make contact with that Mind of your Higher Self.

45. Once you do, then you are able to project them out and perceive them, and give them actual existence in space, in the Now moment. This is the whole reason why it is so important to do everything we can to make contact with our ancestors; either our spiritual or biological ancestors.

46. There are many ways to do this, including praying to them, doing certain rituals, thanking them etc, even something as simple as just thinking about them every night before you go to sleep. Eventually, they will manifest in front of you in one way or another either when awake or asleep.

47. At that time when they do, you are actually projecting them and perceiving them and thus giving them actual existence again in space, in the present, and so they live again. There is nothing they love more than this.

48. So then, to continue about perception. When I move my eyes around, turn my head and look to the side and look behind me, I am bringing all those things I perceive into existence by projecting them from my mind and perceiving them with my senses.

49. The entire process is natural, simple, and effortless because it deals only with vibrations, or thoughts, or we could say images or imaginations. The creation of the universe does not require the expenditure of any energy at all. Energy itself is just another thought in the mind of God.

50. Now of course another obvious question is if creation requires no expenditure of energy, why does it actually take energy to do most anything? Why does it take energy to cook food, walk a mile, drive a car from point A to point B etc?

51. Why can't I just imagine and project the cooked food, or imagine myself in another place and be there? The reason is because the Original Creators set in place natural laws that must be followed in order to have a harmonious, orderly creation.

52. These laws start at the most basic level and go through all seven forms of motion, where a person must crawl before he can walk, walk before he can

run, run before he can fly, fly before he can de-materialize, de-materialize before he can travel mentally, and travel mentally before he can attain total divine unity in which he is everywhere at the same time.

53. As a person develops physically and mentally (spiritually) then he/she discovers higher laws that will supersede the basic laws. At a certain level of development, a person will discover natural laws that will make it possible for him/her to fly instead of walk, or to de-materialize the body and re-materialize somewhere else.

54. The further he/she advances, the less energy he/she will need to do things that require a lot of energy at the basic level, until he/she reaches a stage where he/she can do things without using any energy at all, but simply by using the mind. At that point it is said the person has reached absolute perfection and has become full God like the Elders, lacking them only in experience.

15

OTHER QUESTIONS

The state of Divine Unity is very difficult, if not impossible, to describe in words. It is a state of infiniteness and eternalness, where the mind fully comprehends (and even surpasses) all of infinity and all of eternity.

2. Infinity and eternity, even though they are infinite and eternal, are also the creation of God.

3. They emanate from the mind of God like everything else. So they do not encompass God, but rather God encompasses and even surpasses them. Simply put, God, or the state of Divine Unity, is beyond infinity and eternity.

4. To go even further, God is beyond all concepts, because all concepts emanate from him. And concepts include anything and everything that can be thought, imagined, or enter the mind in any manner. Therefore Divine Unity is that which is unutterable and unimaginable and gives rise to everything utterable and imaginable.

5. To totally understand what this means - what it means to be full God - one has to be full God. It is simply not possible to understand it outside the state of Divine Unity.

6. Maybe a crude example will help to make this clearer. Let us say you are at the top of a high building where you can see the whole city. You have a clear view of all the streets, buildings and even the outskirts of the city and beyond. As soon as you descend back to street level you no longer have this comprehensives view. You are now able to see only individual streets, buildings, etc as far as your vision can go.

7. To get a full comprehensive view of the entire city again, you have to climb to the top of that tallest building once more. But note, even though at street level you cannot see the comprehensive view, once you have seen it, you have the memory

of it in your mind wherever you may be at street level.

8. The same is true with the state of Divine Unity. Once you have experienced it, when you are separated from it you still remember what eternity and infinity are. You are not able to fully explain them with words, but the memory of them remains clear in your mind.

9. The memory that when you were in that state you were beyond infinity and eternity remains with you forever, even after you are separated from the state of Divine Unity.

10. **Brother Blackroots, what is the significance of the speed of the earth around the sun being that it is the number of the beast 66,666 miles per hr?**

11. There is no significance. It turned out that way because it is calculated using the modern calendar and time measurement, which has 24 hours in a day, instead of the ancient calendar which has only 10 hours in a day.

12. Moreover, the modern mile is a bit off compared to the ancient mile. The ancient mile is a bit shorter than the modern mile. It is approximately 86% of the modern mile (exactly 86.2431623%)

13. So if we used the ancient calendar time measurement of 10 hours in one day instead of 24 hours per day, and corrected the modern mile by multiplying it by 0.862431623, then we can recalculate the speed of the earth as follows:

14. 66,666 miles/hr x (24hrs/10hrs) x 0.862431623 and we get approximately:

$$137,987.6797 \text{ miles/hr}$$
(that is ancient miles per ancient hour)

15. In one year or 365.25 days, as the earth makes a full circle around the sun, it will cover a total distance of :
$$137,987.6797 \text{ mi/hr} \times 10 \text{ hrs/day} \times 365.25 \text{ days/year}$$

$$= 504,000,000 \text{ miles}$$

16. That number 504,000,000 you will recognize as the total number of original Gods in the universe, each God united as a man and a woman. When the

Gods separate and incarnate as man and woman the number is:

$$2 \times 504{,}000{,}000 = 1B8M$$

17. So every 2-year cycle, the earth moves around the sun a distance of 1B8M ancient miles.

18. **Peace Brother B, i hope i'm not being disrespectful with this question but i have been wondering about it ever since i met you. Does the initiation bestow you with supernatural powers that you can use like materializing or changing objects etc etc?**

19. Greetings brother _ ,
There is no disrespect my beloved brother. I know this question has been haunting you for a long time, and I knew sooner or later you were going to ask.

20. I also know the real reason you ask is because you want to know whether YOU personally would gain supernatural powers if you were to be initiated. So do not feel any need to apologize - this is a legitimate question that comes into everyone's mind who thinks about initiation.

21. I will answer this way. The true purpose of all initiation is to bring you closer to your First Self. With every ritual you perform successfully, you increase your ability to get into even closer communion with your Higher Self.

22. The Higher Self is all-powerful and all-knowing. The final goal of course is to become one with him/her. Now, along the way there may be certain powers that you inherit from your First Self, and such powers have been used by initiates in the past and present in front of other people.

23. In my case, I have never felt the need to demonstrate any supernatural powers. You may find this unusual, but you see, when I first experienced what it is like to be in close communion with my First Self, the desire to have this communion be a permanent reality was so overwhelming to me that it overshadowed all other desires I had before, including everything I had heard about initiation, even the desire to have so-called supernatural powers.

24. They simply lost their importance to me. I realized from that moment on that if I could become one with the First Self, or at the very least be able to hear the First Self at all times, that

would be the culmination of all my spiritual yearnings. For me it would be the answer to everything.

25. And so all those thoughts I had before about what initiation is all about, and the desires to do miraculous things and so on, were wiped away and replaced by this one desire to unite with my First Self. Ever since my very first major ritual, I have had no other desire go above this one.

26. Now, this does not mean there is anything wrong with being able to perform 'miracles' etc. Everyone's destiny is different. Your Higher Self may lead you along a path where such things are necessary in the course of your spiritual growth.

27. With me, I simply became obsessed with the desire to be just like my First Self, and all other things became secondary. I know that if and when I achieve that final goal, then every thing will be possible for me. The First Self is the fulfillment of all possibilities.

28. So you see, I do not attach that much importance to 'miracles'. To me there really are no miracles, just an understanding and application of

natural laws. And this understanding increases as I get closer and closer to my Higher Self.

That, in a word, is my one and only spiritual goal.

29. **Brother, are there any women thathave been resurrected like the messiahs?**

30. Yes my Sister, there have been many. Mary Magdalene resurrected soon after Jesus. She is his soul mate. All the men in ancient times that have resurrected, their soul mates have also resurrected.

31. See, all these men had very powerful women working with them when they were alive on earth. But these women are hardly ever mentioned at all because we live in an extremely patriarchal society, where people think that only men are important. The fact of the matter is that none of these men would have completed their mission without their women by their side.

32. **If we are gonna resurect in perfect bodies anyway when the judges increase the population, why do we need to fast and meditate etc?**

33. It's important to work on ourselves inside and out in order that we may be able to resurrect consciously while still living. If we do not improve ourselves physically and spiritually through fasting and the exercises in Level 2 of Blackroots Science, then we will not be able to resurrect while still alive.

34. We will die like all other people and our Higher Self will incarnate as another personality in one of the new-born ancient bodies.   Our present personality will go to the ancestral world of Yahweh. It will not take part in the coming reversal on earth.

35. We can be part of the coming reversal only if we resurrect as one of the 144,000 Judges.   Then our present personality will merge with the personality we were before we laid down our bodies as Judges.

36. That ancient Judge personality will take over, and your present personality will be exactly like the personality in your dream that you put aside when you wake up. It will simply become a small part of your ancient personality just like all your dream personalities are a part of you.

37. So this entire lifetime will seem like a dream as we wake up into the true reality of our ancient bodies, exactly like someone who fell asleep, had a long dream, then woke up. The only difference is that we will wake up in the same world we were dreaming about because it is real, not a dream.

38. The only way we can achieve this is if we fast to get our body in a healthy condition, and do the memory exercises to get our minds ready for the conscious resurrection that will make us one of the 144,000.

39. **After the Elohim remove the oxygen you said there will no longer be able to light a fire, is that correct? if so, how will people cook there food in poor countries especially Afrika?**

40. By the time oxygen on earth is replaced with a higher form, there will be new types of plants. These new types will be grown first by people taught by the new Judges. At that time, many of the Judges will have resurrected. They will travel all over the earth to the communities of independent Black people.

41. They will teach them how to grow new plants from the seeds that were stored in pyramids before the beginning of this 6,000-year cycle. There are many varieties of these new plants, and they will be distributed all over the world to all people. The seeds are cultivated for all kinds of climates, from the most arid to the most humid.

42. As I stated before, there are three types of food plants that are needed by the human body. These are the harmonizing plants such as fruits, then the energizing, which are mostly vegetables, and lastly the stabilizing foods, which are grains and beans.

43. Of these three food groups, only fruits are fully developed. By that I mean they develop to 100% right on the tree, and are ready to eat when ripe without the need for cooking.

44. Vegetables on the other hand develop only two-thirds of the way. They need more input of energy in the form of cooking before they are ready to eat. Grains are the least developed. They develop only one-third of the way. So in addition, most grains need more energy input in the form of milling before they can be cooked.

45. The new grains and vegetables that will be grown are able to develop to full maturity just like fruits. The vegetables will be ready to eat right after picking, without the need for cooking. The grains will only need to be soaked in water for a while, then they will be ready to eat without the need for milling or cooking either.

46. There will be so many varieties of these new plants growing all over the earth that food shortage will become a thing of the past. All people will go back to the ancient practice of growing their own food in their communities, and exchanging food with other communities.

47. The whole concept of having food as a commodity for sale will disappear. Food will be so abundant, growing in all types of climates, that hunger will be a thing of the past.

48. Shortly after this, new technologies will be given to these communities, and it will enable them to generate heat and electricity and do many other things without the use of fire or oxygen. So those who like to eat their food hot will be able to do so.

49. Even with this abundance of plant food, there will still be people who cling to the idea of eating

meat. Such people will live in their own secluded private communities, mostly in the north, in Europe. Because of the absence of oxygen, they will not be able to generate electricity or light a fire to cook the meat.

50. Moreover, most of western and eastern Europe and China will be constantly covered by thick clouds for about 300 years. Thus those in the north will not be able to use solar energy either.

51. There will be many new laws also, such as the law prohibiting the building of dams on rivers. These laws will make it impossible for people in the north to generate electricity or heat. So they will be reduced to eating raw meat.

52. Such communities will be very few, and will keep on diminishing. This type of lifestyle will take a toll on their bodies, and their population will diminish more and more as the centuries continue.

53. When their population becomes very small, that will trigger a mutation in the meat-eating animals. They too will begin to disappear and be replaced by new types of animals that can survive only on plants.

54. The mutation of these animals will last the entire 1,000 years or so, till the end of the rule of Yahweh. At the end, there will not be any more animals that prey on other animals or eat meat, except microscopic animalcules.

55. One more thing: Is it true that the extraterrestrials have attempted to wage war against the Elohim? There some legends that I've come across that suggest that they did.

56. When you think about it, how can the et's or anyone for that matter, fight with the Elohim? The Elohim are God in this age. What would be the first thing the et's do to wage war against them?

57. They would have to declare war against God. Let us say for a minute that they do declare war against God, and God chooses to acknowledge them, then what is the next thing they do?

58. They have to go somewhere to find God so they can start their war. The extra-terrestrials had their areas on earth where they lived, and so they could hurl bombs at each other.

59. But the Elohim did not live in a village or town somewhere on earth, so where will the et's go in order to fight with them?

60. The Elohim can find the et's wherever they are located on earth and annihilate them if they want, and the et's cannot retaliate or do anything about it.

61. One of the Elohim can just appear above an et town – with no spaceship – just in his perfect ancient body, suspended in the air over the town, and wave his hand and the entire town will be turned to dust.

62. Or he can wave his hand and turn the entire et population in that location to nothing but hydrogen and oxygen molecules. One minute there could be 100,000 people standing in their town, and the next minute there would not be a single body left, only water flowing downhill – every single one of them turned into water with just one wave of the hand.

63. No my Brother, the et's cannot wage war against the Elohim. When one of the Elohim says to them, I want you off the planet in 14 years, they will be off the planet in 14 years.   That's precisely what happened.

64. One of the Elohim said to them, you will stop your wars immediately and start building interstellar spaceships to leave this planet. I have placed plans in your temples instructing you on how to build them. You will start immediately and do nothing else but this until you finish building them.

65. When you finish, I will show you how to travel to your new homes in the star systems I have prepared for you. You will travel there when your spaceships are ready, and you will not come back to earth until I give you permission.

66. That was not a negotiation. It was an order from God to his creatures, and they obeyed. They used the plans God gave them to build their spaceships.

67. Within a period of 14 years, they had completed building their star ships. The Elohim had already completed much of the preparation for them on these planets, which already had water, plants and animals, but were not occupied by humans.

68. When they were ready to leave, the Elohim provided them with star maps and taught them how to travel through the various portals shown on the maps in order to reach their new homes.

69. So the et's were gone within a period of 14 years after the end of their wars against each other on earth.

70. After reaching their new homes, they promptly resumed their wars with one another, but those also ended very quickly when they all developed the technology to totally destroy each other.

71. The only ones left on earth were the Annunaki, who were allowed to remain for another 200 years, after which they were also ordered to leave.

16

HOW TO GET RID OF HARMFUL THOUGHTS

Harmful thoughts are all the thoughts that do not help you to advance closer to your First Self. Not only that, but they actually retard your progress, causing you to move further away from your First Self.

2. These thoughts can come in many forms. Some are brought on by your learnt inferiority complex (children are not born with an inferiority complex, but learn it from adults), others come out of bad mental habits practiced over many years.

3. Let us use as an example a thought that occurs among some black men that they do not want to talk about. That is the desire that some black men have for white women.

4. Nowadays this is a taboo subject among black people as more and more are awakening from their 6,000 year slumber. But some still find it difficult to overcome this desire, and so they hide it, pretending that they are no longer attracted to these light race women.

5. There is a very simple way to get rid of these thoughts and desires. All you have to do every time such an unwanted thought or desire forces itself into your mind, is to say,

6. "I take this unwanted thought (or desire) and I am putting it in a trash bag and dumping it in the Most High's trash can. My Higher Self will get rid of it for me, and in exchange will replace it in my mind with an infinitely more wholesome and balanced thought".

7. So every time you see a light race woman that attracts you, use that phrase. Imagine yourself putting that woman in a trash bag and dumping her in a trash can.

8.   In exchange, imagine God giving you an infinitely more wholesome, beautiful and decent woman who is meant just for you; i.e. your eternal soul mate.

9.   This mental act will work for every unwholesome thought or desire that enters your mind.   Simply dump it and imagine yourself receiving the replacement from your Higher Self, which will exceed that bad thought by an infinite amount, because it is true that what you will receive from your Higher Self will be infinitely better.

10.   Rest assured that if you do this, your Higher Self will indeed reward you.   He/She is already waiting for you to do it.

11.   And I want to repeat that this ALWAYS works. You don't have to take my word for it.   All you have to do is try it and see for yourself.